To Mum and Dad for all their love,
support and encouragement

PLAYING WITH THE BOYS

By
NIAMH McKEVITT

VSP

Published by Vision Sports Publishing in 2015

Vision Sports Publishing
19-23 High Street
Kingston upon Thames
Surrey
KT1 1LL

www.visionsp.co.uk

ISBN: 978-1909534-38-4

A CIP record for this book is available from the British library

Written by Niamh McKevitt, with Steve McKevitt
Managing editor: Jim Drewett
Editor: Paul Baillie-Lane
Cover design: Neal Cobourne
Back cover photgraph: Shaun Bloodworth

Printed and bound in the UK by TJ International, Padstow, Cornwall

MIX
Paper from
responsible sources
FSC® C013056

CONTENTS

Acknowledgements

So many people have helped me along the way, but I'd like to give special thanks to the following people (in chronological order):

Fiona McKevitt, my mum
Steve McKevitt, my dad, who wrote the book with me
Evan McKevitt for getting the whole thing started
Marcus Brameld, Community Manager, Sheffield Wednesday FC
Kevin Noteman, Coach, Sheffield Wednesday FC
Craig Thomson, Coach, Sheffield Wednesday FC
Richard Sykes, Manager, Sheffield Wednesday Ladies FC
Russ Lymm, Coach, Sheffield Wednesday Ladies FC
Richard Stevenson, Coach, Sheffield Wednesday Boys EPDC
Iain Lothian, Manager, Millhouses Juniors Boys JFC
Pete Harper, Head Coach, South Yorkshire Schools County FA
Glen Preston, First Team Manager, Huddersfield Town Ladies FC
Steve Featherstone, Head Coach, Beighton Magpies Boys JFC

For their work in promoting mixed football and allowing me to play:

Rachel Pavlou, National Women's Development Officer, the Football Association
Dr Laura Hills, Senior Lecturer in Youth Sport, Brunel University, London

For their generosity:

Frank Carolan and Rob Brealey at Golden (I'm still wearing the boots)

And last, but not least, Sheffield Wednesday Ladies' amazing under 9s squad 2014/15:

Libby Andrew
Scarlett Anson
Maisy Martin
Gracie McGregor
Aoife McKevitt
Leila Saleh
Ellie Wright

Disclaimer:
All the people and events described in this book are real, but some of the names have been changed. All the events have been described exactly as I remember them.

Preface

As we line up for the kick-off I'm on the side of the pitch near all the parents and friends who have come to watch the match. I can see my dad in the crowd. This is an under 14s match in the top division of the Sheffield & District Boys League: the biggest junior football league in Europe. I'm the only girl on the pitch.

The supporters of our opponents, Sheffield Wednesday Young Owls, the current league leaders, have noticed me now. I can hear them laughing. One of them shouts to their striker, "Hey Rudi, make sure you get the full-back's phone number when you go past her!"

Rudi laughs too. He thinks this is going to be easy. Young Owls are a big side and Rudi is their biggest player. He's about 6ft tall and must be 11st. In fact he looks a bit overweight to me.

Dad's heard them as well.

"What a surprise Niamh, they're laughing at you."

He smiles at me.

"I know," I say and smile back.

I tell myself the jokes mean that Rudi will be complacent because I'm a girl and I'm determined to use that to my advantage.

I get my chance almost straight away. From the kick-off Rudi picks up a pass on the left and pokes the ball past Luke in left-midfield. I notice he moves well for a big guy, but he's slightly over-hit the ball and I know I can get there. I charge into the sliding tackle as hard as I can. Rudi might be quick but he wasn't expecting this. Bang! I get the ball but take the man out too. The ball goes out of play and Rudi flies through the air and falls to the ground with a heavy thump. He looks winded. The supporters start shouting at the referee, calling for a free kick. So does Rudi. But the ref ignores them and says, "Throw-in. Get on with it."

Rudi gets up and I go over and mark him. He still looks a bit dazed, like he can't believe what's just happened, but he's okay.

"Sorry mate," I say lightly. "You were just a bit too quick for me."

I notice he's limping slightly for a few minutes afterwards.

"That was a sick tackle," says Sheriyar, who's filling in for Ben at centre-back. "He didn't know what hit him!"

The next time Rudi gets the ball on the left he comes towards me. I stand side-on, showing him – daring him – to go down the left. He hesitates. I can tell he's worried about getting clattered again. He decides against it, brings the ball onto his weaker right foot and plays it square. In that moment I know I've got him. I know he's not getting past me today.

I wonder if he still wants my number...

Chapter 1
The Ice Man Cometh

"I like my women to be feminine, not sliding into tackles and covered in mud."
Brian Clough

When I was five years old I asked my dad why he liked football so much. He seemed to spend all his time either playing or watching it. Without hesitating, he said it was because it was the greatest game in the world. But I couldn't see it. It looked pretty boring to me. I was much more interested in princesses and dolls.

Mum was working nights at the time, so every Tuesday evening Dad took my little brother Evan and me to 'watch' him play five-a-side football. In fact, I took very little notice. Dad would sit us behind one of the goals and warn us not to move. At first I sat reading a book or playing with a doll, while Evan acted out World War III on the astroturf with his soldiers. After a while we both got bored and started playing about at the side of the pitch with one of the spare match balls. Dad said he was very pleased to see us do that. As the weeks went on we stopped bringing our toys and just played with the football instead.

At the time I thought Evan was taking no notice either, but he must have been because he told his teacher, all his classmates and several parents that Dad was a Premier League footballer who played for Wigan Athletic. Dad, who was 38 at the time, was visibly shocked when he came to pick us up from school one day and someone asked him for his autograph. He had to explain that he actually played in the 'Premier League' at 'Goals Five-a-Side Soccer'... in a Wigan top.

Evan continued to show some interest in football so Dad started taking him to Sheffield Wednesday Soccer Skills on Saturday mornings. One week Mum was working so I had to go along too. We stood on the side with the other parents watching the boys play. It was a bit tedious so Dad got one of the spare balls and we passed it to each other on the sidelines. Unfortunately before long the coaches needed it for one of the drills, so we had to stand and watch again.

"You should just join in," said Dad. "It would be better than standing here with me."

I hadn't thought about actually playing before, but Evan seemed to be having fun so I decided that next week I would play too. When we turned up the following Saturday a lot of the boys – and there were only boys – were much older than me and seemed twice my size. I was genuinely scared and spent the first session hiding in the far corners of the pitch, trying to stay away from the biggest boys and – most importantly – from the ball.

The soccer school was run by Marcus Brameld, who was the community officer at Sheffield Wednesday and a senior coach at their academy. Marcus had been a youth player at Manchester United. He was helped by two other academy coaches: Kev and Tommo. Kev had played for Leeds and Doncaster Rovers while Tommo had played at Rotherham. They all made me feel really welcome.

"We need more girls playing football, so make sure you keep coming," said Tommo.

Kev asked me if I'd ever done any dancing. I told him I used to do ballet on Saturday mornings.

"I thought so. I'm not joking, but that has really helped with your movement. Rio Ferdinand did ballet until he was 16. In a few weeks you'll be dancing round this lot."

I didn't know who Rio Ferdinand was, but it sounded encouraging.

If it wasn't for the coaches, that first session could have been one of the longest hours of my life. I really didn't take to it at all. I had very little natural ability – I could only really kick the ball when it wasn't moving – although surprisingly I wasn't the worst player there by any means.

On the way home after only my second week, I asked if I could stop going to football. Dad told me that I could pack it in if I liked, but I should try and give it a few weeks at least. He said that if I carried on I'd get better quite quickly and would start to enjoy it much more. I didn't believe him, but Evan was still going and the only alternative was doing the weekly supermarket shop with my mum, so I agreed to stick it out for four more weeks and see how I felt then.

In the first month I don't think I got noticeably better, but suddenly things began clicking into place. I started being able to kick the ball properly and learned to control it and how to pass. Looking back, the coaching really was excellent: the best introduction to the game anyone could have hoped for.

It wasn't bad being the only girl – well, at least not until the end of the session when it came to picking the sides for a match. For ages I'd always get picked last. This used to annoy me so much that I would always have it in for the opposing team's captain. The most embarrassing time was when it was a final choice between me and a tiny four-year-old boy. I'd been playing for a year by now and it was his first week. Not only that, but he'd obviously never played before. He kept trying to pick the ball up and didn't really seem to know where he was. The Sheffield United shirt he was wearing had several years' growth in it and it trailed round his ankles like a dress. Hughie, the captain, chose the four-year-old boy instead of me.

"There's no way I'm picking that girl!" I heard him say to Tommo.

I was furious and made it my personal aim to tackle Hughie as hard as I could during the match. After a few minutes he came running down the wing – my wing – and I had my chance. I ran towards him as fast as I could, determined to win the challenge, but at the last moment I backed out and simply collided with him instead. I fell to the ground as he emerged with the ball and scored. I was really angry with myself. It had been my one opportunity for revenge and I'd blown it, and that had hurt even more than being picked last. I promised myself that I wouldn't back out of a tackle again.

Sometimes my presence caused some unexpected problems. One week the coaches set up a drill which involved two players going in goal. The two goalkeepers had to hold hands, which was supposed to improve communication and positioning, because rather than just going where we wanted we'd have to talk to each other and work as a team. At least we would've done if my partner, Jack, hadn't refused to hold hands with me.

Jack looked horrified at the prospect of holding a girl's hand and when our turn came, he physically recoiled from my outstretched palm. No amount of cajoling from the coaches could persuade him and he actually held his own hands behind his back just to make sure I didn't grab them by surprise. In the end a compromise was reached and we held on to either end of a training bib. Jack seemed satisfied with that and with physical contact avoided, his honour was maintained. (To tell the truth, I wasn't very keen on holding his hand either.)

At the end of each session Kev and Tommo would pick the best player and present them with a trophy to take home for the week. It was a clear, plastic figurine of a footballer on a marble plinth, so we called it the 'Ice Man'. Being carted off to a different kid's home every week meant that the Ice Man had seen better days, but we really loved it. Marcus once tried to change the now armless Ice Man for a more robust shield, but we demanded the original's return and he was back the following week.

I'll never forget the first time I won the Ice Man. I'd scored the winning goal in the five-a-side match and managed to do a drag-back. I thought I'd played pretty well and there were a few words of encouragment from Kev and Tommo, but I still didn't expect to be picked out. However, when Tommo said, "This week the Ice Man goes to the player who scored a brilliant goal and did a great skill…" I realised it was me. The boys clapped as I went to get the trophy and it felt like I'd been officially accepted as part of the group.

That's one of the things I've noticed over the years: the better players in the team always seem to hang out together. It was the first time I'd encountered this, but it's been the same everywhere I've played: no one really talks to you until you've earned their respect and they regard you as 'a player'. After I won the Ice Man, some of the better players started talking to me and I was never picked last again.

Marcus regularly asked me if any of my friends fancied coming down to play ("We need more girls playing, Niamh," he said) and he would give me some leaflets to hand out in school. My teacher pinned one up on the noticeboard and several boys from my school, including a couple in my class – Dan and Matthew – started coming too. One or two girls did check it out, but most of them gave up after a couple of weeks.

But I was enjoying football more and more and looking for every opportunity to play. I began playing after school on Wednesday evenings, but Sheffield Wednesday Soccer Skills was the highlight of the week.

As the summer holidays approached, Kev handed out some leaflets for a soccer camp that he was running with Tommo at a local school. Playing football for the whole day sounded great. I really wanted to go.

On the morning of the first day, Mum dropped Evan and me off in reception and Kev told us both to go and wait in the changing room. We walked round the corner and there was a boys' changing room and a girls' changing room. The door to the boys' room was ajar and they looked shocked to think that I might walk in on them.

"There's a girl! You can't come in here!" someone shouted.

'Fine,' I thought, 'I'll go and wait in the girls' changing room'. So I did.

There was no one else in there and some of the boys kept knocking on the door and running away, which was quite annoying. After about 10 minutes Tommo opened the door and asked me what I was doing sat on my own and invited me into the other changing room. Of course, everyone had turned up in their kit: nobody was getting changed at all.

"But that's a girl!" said one of the knock-and-run boys.

"Nothing wrong with your eyesight is there, Conor?" said Kev. "Her name's Niamh and she's agreed to come along to help me and Tommo teach you lot how to play football."

Over the next two years I steadily improved to become one of the 'average' players in the group. I was so proud to be average. I was almost always the only girl there, so being regarded as a regular player by the boys felt like something of an achievement.

One week, Marcus asked me and another boy, Jacob, if we'd like to join him while he was coaching the older age group. Jacob didn't like playing with the bigger lads, so he went back to the younger group after five minutes, leaving me on my own. I wasn't sure what to do but Dad said he'd stay and watch and I'd be fine. In the match at the end, I was put in defence and one of the older lads started bossing me about.

"Ignore Tom," said Marcus. "He doesn't know what he's talking about. Just listen to me."

I thought I'd played quite well because no one got past me. I just did whatever Marcus told me.

At the end he said: "Right, Man of the Match this week

is easy. It's actually Player of the Week because it's Niamh. You were like John Terry at the back there. Well done!"

I felt really proud when all the boys clapped as I picked up the trophy.

Afterwards Marcus asked if he could have a word with my dad. He said I was progressing really well and wondered if I fancied playing for a proper team. I'd never thought about making that move before, but without hesitation I said 'yes'. Then he told us that he had recommended me to Sheffield Wednesday Ladies and had arranged for me to go for a trial the following week.

Dad said that the trial was a very good opportunity, but I was actually a little bit disappointed because I supported Sheffield United – couldn't I play for them instead? Dad laughed and said it didn't work like that.

"Don't worry, Niamh. I think half of the Sheffield Wednesday Boys' Academy are actually Blades," said Marcus.

Both he and Dad said it would be a good experience to go along and try out to see how I got on.

"You've got nothing to lose. And if you don't like it you can always carry on coming here," said Marcus.

I was very nervous when the day of my trial arrived. I was quite shy at that age but I expected the other players would be friendly and come over and welcome me. I have since learned that being shy doesn't really get you anywhere other than overlooked. Naturally, they just ignored me completely. There were around 25 girls there. Some of them were quite loud and it was clear that a few had played together before.

The trial was split into two halves: a skills session and a practice match. I struggled with the skills, especially the heading drill because I closed my eyes when the ball came at me and succeeded in missing it every single time. I was a bit embarrassed and during the break asked Dad if we could just go home and give it all up as a bad idea. He said

I should wait and see what happened in the match, as that was the most important part. He told me to be brave and just do my best.

Before dividing us into teams for the game, Richard, the manager, asked us what our favoured positions were. He asked if there were any defenders and I said I was. I noticed that no one else did. The sides were split into 'Probables' – containing all the girls who'd played the previous season along with the best trialists – against 'Possibles', which were the rest of us.

The result was never really in doubt, but something remarkable happened. Straight from the kick-off, one of the opposition strikers came running towards me with the ball. This time I knew what to do and I didn't chicken out. I went in for the tackle, won the ball fairly and passed it to one of my team-mates. I managed to win the ball three or four more times during the rest of the game and each time either kicked it out or passed it to one of my team (which was a major achievement for me). After the match, I asked Dad how he thought I'd done.

"To be honest, the first session wasn't great and you looked like one of the weaker players there. The match was a big surprise, though. I don't know what happened at the kick-off, but you appeared to turn into Bobby Moore."

I didn't know who Bobby Moore was, but it sounded like I'd done okay. A few hours later Richard rang to say that I'd been successful and, if I wanted to, I could join the squad. I was the only 'Possible' to be offered a place. I was put into the under 10s team, rather than the under 9s, even though I was only eight. Richard said he thought it would be more challenging and the fact that I'd been training with boys would mean I'd be able cope with the physical side of playing a year up.

I was so pleased to get into a team, but I couldn't really share this news with my school friends. None of the girls in my class were remotely interested in football. Quite a few of the boys were playing for teams at the weekends too, but I was never able to join in with their conversations. They didn't take girls' football seriously, so I certainly couldn't talk to anyone about anything that happened at Wednesday.

My first big disappointment in football came at the age of 10 when I tried out for the school team. It was my final year of primary school. At the start of the autumn term all the boys received a letter saying that there would be after-school football training on Wednesdays, from which a school seven-a-side team would be chosen. I asked the teacher for a letter too and Mum and Dad said I could go along.

Obviously, I was the only girl there. The school had hired a professional football coach called Mr Toy, who was involved with Rotherham United, to run the training and pick the team. I'd imagined he'd look a bit like Kev or Tommo: like a professional footballer but a bit older. In real life he was actually much older than any footballer I'd ever seen and, without being mean, he was quite a lot bigger as well. He didn't look like he'd played football in a long time. Mr Toy was also very strict and, unlike Tommo and Kev, wasn't very friendly at all. He began by gathering us together in the middle of the pitch.

"Right lads, I want to split you into two groups. Can all of you who already play for a team – 'the footballers' – stand in that goal and anyone who doesn't – 'the non-footballers' – go and stand in the other one."

I went to stand with all the boys who played for teams. There were eight of us in the 'footballers' group, which contained all the better players. Mr Toy looked at both groups.

"Right, I'm going to mix things up a bit," he said.

He pointed at Alex, the biggest boy in our year, who was standing with the 'non-footballers'.

"Could you come over to this side."

Then he pointed at me.

"And could you go over there, please."

That seemed to be the end of the mixing up. I was quite upset, but I didn't say anything. For the rest of the session Mr Toy trained the boys in the 'footballers' group while the 'non-footballers' trained with our P.E teacher, Mr Breilsford. Some of the boys in my group weren't too bad in the drills, but when we played a match against the 'footballers' at the end, the fact that no one else played for a team meant that they didn't know how to stay in position or where to stand. I tried to tell them, but it was really just me on my own at the back against two or three strikers. We got hammered.

After the game Mr Toy said that we'd all played well and that the 'footballers' group would now be the school team. He also said that there was one more place left and, to decide who would get it, there would be a raffle during lunchtime the following day, when the name of one of the 'non-footballers' would be pulled out of a hat.

When I got home Dad asked me how it had gone. He got quite angry when I told him what had happened. He said he was going to go into the school the next day to "have it out with that coach." I told him there was no point as Mr Toy wasn't actually a teacher and so he wouldn't be there. Mum said she thought it would better if she dealt with it and she was probably right.

Mum had a meeting with Mr Breilsford, who said that he wasn't actually picking the team but that he didn't think girls were allowed to play for 'insurance reasons'. Mum told Mr Breilsford that she had already contacted the Football Association and this wasn't true. Mixed football – boys and girls playing in the same team – was allowed up to the age of 11. Mr Breilsford said he'd have a think about it and talk to Mr Toy.

It was a few days before Mr Breilsford sent Mum an email

which said that there was good news and bad news. The good news was that they were going to start a girls' team and I could play in that. With that in mind, as far as the boys' team was concerned, the bad news was that Mr Toy's decision was final and they didn't think it was fair that a boy should miss out on a place because of me now I had a girls' football team I could play in.

This still seemed really unfair to me. My dad said that he agreed but that there was nothing we could do about it because, in the end, Mr Toy would just say, "Sorry, but I just don't think she's good enough," and we couldn't argue with that. Dad also said he wished he could tell me that this would never happen to me again, but unfortunately it would.

"Try to think of it as a manager whose plans you don't fit into," he reassured me. "Lots of players are released by one club because they're supposedly not good enough, but go on to be brilliant at a different club. Just because Mr Toy doesn't want you doesn't mean you're not a good player."

To be fair to Mr Breilsford, he was as good as his word and he did start a girls' team. While it was nice to play with my friends, it was clear from the first training session that hardly any of them had ever kicked a ball before, let alone played a match. But at least we had a team. Mr Breilsford entered us into a schoolgirls' five-a-side tournament and asked if any parents would be willing to help out. Dad offered to come along.

I was the only member of the team who'd played before, so none of the other girls even had a pair of football boots. My feet grew really quickly when I was young (they're size 8 now, but thankfully seem to have stopped) and I was going through new pairs of boots every three months. We brought five of my old pairs with us and when we arrived my dad gathered the girls round and handed them out. He asked if anyone had played football before. Two said they'd played a bit with their brothers.

The other teams were like us. Most consisted of only one or two girls who'd played before and five or six novices. The good players tended to cancel each other out and very few goals were scored. Dad and Mr Breilsford got us organised into basic positions and our first two matches finished 0-0. At the end of the second game, they gave a team talk and said we were doing really well and could be proud of the fact that we were unbeaten. But Mr Breilsford noticed Hayley looking unhappy.

"What's wrong, Hayley?"

"It's just that we've had the day off school to come here and we haven't even scored a goal," she replied. "I'm very worried that we'll have nothing to say tomorrow at Good Work Assembly."

Dad nodded in sympathy and said, "I believe Wayne Rooney starts every game with very similar concerns, Hayley. Look girls – a win would take us into the quarter-finals. That would be a real achievement considering most of you have never played before. All you need to do is score one goal."

But how? Just before our final match Dad told me he'd had an idea.

"I've been watching these games. It's obvious that most of the goalkeepers have never played before. You've got a great throw on you. So if we do win a throw-in, I want you to aim it as hard as you can at the goal. The keeper will try to save it and if they touch the ball before it goes in then it'll be a goal."

It seemed like a good idea to me and, with about five minutes of the last game to go, we got a throw-in just inside the opposition's half and I had my chance.

"Launch one, Niamh!" shouted Dad.

I took a run-up and, instead of throwing it to a team-mate, I aimed it as hard as I could just above the keeper's head. She was taken by surprise and, although she managed to get her hands up, could only palm the ball into the roof of the net. The players and the teachers all looked at the referee. She seemed to think about it for a moment and then pointed at the centre circle, indicating a goal.

The rest of my team dived on me and started cheering. Dad and Mr Breilsford were jumping up and down and the teachers from the other school were arguing with the ref, but she just shrugged and told them to get on with the game. The goal stood. It might have been a bit unconventional but I didn't care: I had just scored my first ever goal in a proper match. We hung on to win the game, but unfortunately we went out on penalties in the quarter-final. It was a huge achievement nonetheless.

It had been fun, but it hadn't really been the kind of school football I was after. I still wanted to play for the boys' team and I knew I was good enough. All I wanted was a chance to prove it, but there didn't seem to be any way that that was going to happen.

Chapter 2
Girls on Top

"Tomboy. Alright, call me a tomboy. Tomboys get medals. Tomboys win championships. Tomboys can fly. Oh, and tomboys aren't boys."
Julie Foudy, former US footballer who finished her career with 271 caps

Sheffield Wednesday Ladies is one of the biggest grassroots women's clubs in the country. There are girls' teams at every age group from under 9s through to under 18s and three adult sides competing from County up to Regional level. The junior teams play in the Sheffield and Hallamshire League, which claims to be both the oldest and largest girls' league in the country.

In my first proper season with Wednesday Under 10s, our league consisted of 15 teams split into two divisions (we played in the top flight: the A League). Matches were seven-a-side, with most clubs having squads of nine or 10 players. The equivalent boys' league had 79 teams in seven divisions. What's more, although they also played seven-a-side, the boys fielded two teams with the aggregate score over two matches giving the result, so there could easily be 18 players in each squad.

Girls' football might be the fastest growing sport in the UK, but compared with the boys the number of players is tiny and so it is still a minority sport. I think this is one of the reasons why boys are generally considered to be better at it than girls: because there are larger numbers of them playing there's much more competition.

Another reason is that a lot of girls just play football for fun. By that I mean it's often just one of a number of pastimes – along with say, dancing or Brownies – rather than their sole focus. Being great at football is a big deal if you're a boy, but if you're a girl most of your friends are unlikely to play the game and couldn't care less how good you are at it. It's not really something to shout about; it's just 'a thing' to do on Saturday mornings. So, when the training night was announced, I was very sad at first because it clashed with Brownies and I didn't want to give that up. But I'd never played in an actual match at that point and Dad told me I'd enjoy that more than I could imagine.

"Believe me, as soon as you've finished one game you'll want to play another straight away," he said.

I remember getting really angry with him when he told me that, thinking that it was a ridiculous thing to say. I mean, what could possibly be better than Brownies?

As it turned out, the answer was 'playing in football matches'. And fortunately there were plenty of games. Playing football with Wednesday really was fun and Richard and Russ proved to be really good coaches. They concentrated on getting us to pass the ball about and taught us how to play in position. We lost our first few games but steadily improved and learned how to play as a team. We ended up finishing third, beating every team in the league at least once. I grew to really enjoy the rhythm of training on a Wednesday evening and playing a match on Saturday morning, which was now established as the centrepiece of my week.

Richard and Russ put loads of effort into running the team. On top of all the league matches, they were always looking for tournaments and competitions for us to enter or friendlies to play in. We even became regional futsal champions and went to the national finals at the English Institute of Sport.

Richard also arranged matches with boys' teams to give

us an extra challenge. Some of the parents weren't as keen on this, but I really looked forward to them. The best team we played were a side called Sheffield Sixes. They were top of their league and were really cocky when they turned up. I didn't know it at the time, but I would have several encounters with Sixes over the coming years.

Before this game their manager came over to tell us not to worry because he'd told the lads to "go easy on us." Richard thanked him and replied, in that case, he'd tell us to go easy on them too. Their manager laughed as if that was the funniest thing he'd ever heard. You could tell they weren't taking it seriously; it was just a glorified training session for them.

As we were getting ready to kick-off, one of the boys said, "I'm not tackling any girls." To which one of his team-mates replied, "Don't worry, you won't have to!"

There was lots more laughter and although I didn't know how anyone else felt, I was really annoyed by this. I played football with boys every day in the school playground and certainly wasn't scared of this lot. Sixes obviously thought they were going to murder us. They were a good side but we were playing on astroturf, which I think suited our game much better. There were no sliding tackles and the surface allowed us to pass it about quickly. The lads were, player for player, probably more skilful than we were, but they didn't play as well as a team. They kept trying to run at us, keeping hold of the ball for too long and playing themselves into trouble. Looking back, I find it's always easier to defend if you know the kid you're up against is definitely not going to pass. You just run them into the corner.

And I think their complacent attitude really helped us because we beat them 2-0. We scored quite early in the match and they got more and more frustrated as the game went on. By the end of the match nobody was going easy on anyone. We scored the second goal with a few minutes to go and you could tell that it finished them. I made sure I shook hands with every one of them at the end and really enjoyed smiling nicely and saying, "Hard luck, mate!" To have beaten them felt like a real achievement.

After it was over their manager was really nice. He was laughing with Richard and Russ and saying how his lads had been taken by surprise. He told us we'd done really well and that he was genuinely impressed. He joked that he was glad we weren't playing in the same league.

Sixes had a good reputation and for the first time ever the boys in school were impressed by something one of my teams had done. Prior to that there hadn't really been any nasty comments as such, it was more that they just didn't take me seriously. I knew I could play as well as the boys, but they didn't seem to get that.

Whenever I got on the ball in these playground matches someone would shout, "The girl's got the ball! The girl's got the ball!" as if I'd stolen their property or some miracle had happened. Others found the whole idea of a girl playing a bit of a joke and the novelty didn't wear off as fast as I'd have liked. It was as if they'd been brought up to believe that girls can't play football, in the same way that fish can't ride bicycles.

I often wondered what would have happened if Wednesday Ladies Under 10s had entered the boys' league. I think we would have done well, but unfortunately that was to be the only season we all played together. A new chairman was in charge at the club and he fell out with Richard and Russ. He was insisting that we must all play in our own age group the following season.

Not only did I really rate Richard and Russ, but I really liked playing for them. They gave me so much confidence. Along with three of my team-mates, I opted to move on with them to a new club, Middlewood Rovers, where we could play at under 11 level. It was an easy decision for me, but for a while it seemed like it might have been a mistake because we only managed to scrape together eight players. Again, this shows how few girls there are playing football. I was still at primary school but I'd already been playing for four years. The rest of the Rovers team had been playing even longer. If I was to invite one of my friends along who'd never played before, they'd have had too much ground to make up, even at that age.

This is not a problem you would encounter in boys' football. While there are of course lots of boys in this age group who have never played for a team before either, many of those will have watched football, either live or on TV, and would have mastered the basics of kicking/passing/shooting and heading in parks, playgrounds and back gardens. However, there's not really a comparable culture of girls going down the park for a kickabout.

Heading is another of the major differences between the boys' and the girls' game. A lot of girls won't head the ball, but I've got my dad to 'thank' for the fact that I'm not one of them. Before the season with Rovers started, we arrived at heading in his programme of one-on-one coaching.

"You can't be a good defender unless you can head the ball," Dad told me.

Our weekly trips to the park were now spent exclusively practicing heading.

"If you do it properly, you won't feel any pain," he lied.

These training sessions consisted – it seemed to me – of him blasting the ball at me as hard as he could from 20 metres away (he called it 'crossing') and then making me run to fetch it if I didn't head it past Evan, who was in goal.

"It doesn't hurt," he'd claim, when I occasionally managed to make contact with what felt like a sphere of solid iron.

"Yes it does!" I'd shout back through my migraine.

We'd only be allowed to go home if I did three, five or ten

in a row. It was a very long summer.

Dad later told me that he used to get very strange looks from the other parents in the park due to the obvious torture he was inflicting on a small child, but eventually I became brave enough to head it no matter how high he kicked it. It's actually quite exhilarating heading the ball – and when you do it in a game it's always followed by shouts of 'Well done!' from the touchline.

My second season in girls' football was even better than the first. Fixtures began in September and we won 15 league and cup matches on the run. We didn't drop a point until March the following year. It wasn't a procession though. It's very difficult for a girls' team to pick up new squad members. We were a seven-a-side team with a squad of only eight players. If someone was injured or ill, which they often were, we'd have to play without a sub.

Things really came to a head in the semi-final of the cup. Two of our players, Fran and Libby, were due to play at Wembley for their school team in the final of a national tournament on the same day. That was great for them, but it meant they would miss the game, leaving us with just six players and no goalkeeper. What's worse, we were up against a really good team, Worksop Town, who we'd only narrowly beaten in the league with a full squad.

It was an amazing match to play in. We did nothing but defend and tried to pass the ball to Amy (our entire midfield) or hit it over the top for Bridie (our only striker) to chase. After an initial period of pressure from Worksop, we managed to get into the game more and more and kept the score at 0-0. In the last minute of extra time, when it looked certain the match would go to penalties, we cleared the ball to Amy on the right, where she beat the defender and crossed it into the middle. It fell to Bridie, who volleyed the ball into the roof of the net. It was an amazing goal and, with barely enough time for the restart, proved to be the winner.

Winning that semi-final was one of the happiest moments of my life. At the final whistle all the parents ran onto the pitch and lifted us into the air. Everyone was jumping and cheering – it was like we'd actually won the cup rather than a semi-final. My granddad, who had come to watch me for the first time, was amazed. He'd coached boys' teams for years, but said he would never have believed girls could be, "So technically good at such a young age".

We finished our first season at Rovers as league and cup winners. I felt I'd really improved as a player. At school, however, even though I played with them in the playground every day, I was still not really taken seriously by some of the lads. One time the boy whose ball it was wouldn't let me join in. It all started because I'd been picked before him and some of the other boys were taking the mickey. He got angry and said football wasn't a game for girls or sissies and pushed me over.

And that's how my first (and, to this day, only) fight started. I got up, told him to "Piss off!" and joined in anyway. But then he said he was going to tell the teacher on me for swearing and I just lost it. I ran after him, pushed him over and we started fighting. I was punching him (probably not very hard) and shouting, "Is this sissy enough for you?"

I got into trouble for that but he didn't try to stop me playing again.

The football season was over, but Mr Breilsford told us that he had entered both the boys' and girls' school teams into a summer tournament that would be played at Bramall Lane, the home ground of my team, Sheffield United. He asked me if my dad would be willing to help out again because the tournament was being played on a Sunday and Mr Toy wouldn't be able to attend.

The playing area was divided into six five-a-side pitches.

In the boys' tournament there were 25 teams split into five groups. Meanwhile, just three other schools had entered the girls' tournament.

We won our first match 6-0. I scored all six goals but it wasn't much of an achievement really. The other team didn't know how to mark-up or where to stand at goalkicks. Every time the opposition got a goalkick I could tell where their goalkeeper was going to kick the ball, so I intercepted it and scored. It was much better than a corner. I played in goal for our next game, which we drew 0-0, and scored both goals in our final match, a 2-2 draw. And that was that. We were all done in less than an hour.

Dad found Mr Breilsford and told him we were all leaving.

"It was a bit of a non-event to be honest, John," said Dad. "I think the girls were just getting into it when it was all over."

"I can't believe it," said Mr Breilsford, "the lads have only played one game. We've got the second one in 10 minutes."

He paused for a moment. "Have you got to go now or can you stick around for a bit?"

Dad said we didn't have to be anywhere.

"Hey lads," said Mr Breilsford. "What do you reckon we let Niamh join us for the rest of the day?"

To my utter surprise the boys all said 'yes' instantly. I was so happy. I was finally going to get to play for the school team. Thank goodness Mr Toy couldn't make it!

As the tournament progressed I thought I was doing okay. I was managing to get in quite a few winning tackles. I realised that the boys from opposing teams weren't expecting me to challenge them, which actually made it a bit easier than normal. We seemed to be getting the biggest crowds too. I guess a lot of people were curious to see a girl playing and the neutrals seemed to be cheering us on more than the teams we were playing against. I felt really comfortable. The standard wasn't amazing though, and certainly none of the school teams we played were as good as Sheffield Sixes.

I thought our school team was pretty good, but probably not as good as Rovers. If the two teams had played against each other I'd have backed Rovers to win. The big difference between boys' and girls' football was not between the individual players, but in the *overall* standard. Rovers were by far the best girls' team in the county. There were two or three teams who could give us a game, but that was it. What struck me most at this tournament was that a majority of the boys playing were pretty decent, so it was a lot more competitive. I really enjoyed that aspect of it.

Dad said he thought I'd done okay and hadn't looked out of place. I was really pleased with that, but disappointed at the same time. I'd have loved to carry on playing, but this was literally the last game for the school team, as we were all leaving for secondary school in a few weeks.

As we made our way out, we saw a woman in a tracksuit coming towards us. She introduced herself as Gemma and said she was a woman's development officer at the FA. She asked me if I'd be interested in going for a trial at the Sheffield United Girls' Centre of Excellence (CoE). I said I didn't really know what that was.

"It's an academy for elite female footballers. They are run regionally by the FA," said Gemma. "Sheffield United have four teams at under 11, under 13, under 15 and under 17, and also a development squad. The centre is all about developing players and all the coaching is done by qualified UEFA coaches. I can arrange a trial for you there if you'd like?"

Gemma gave Dad her number and he said we'd have a chat about it. It sounded really good, but I really wasn't sure that I wanted to leave Rovers. However, I think it is always better to try things out before making a decision, so we contacted Gemma and she put us in touch with the Sheffield United Girls' CoE.

Chapter 3

ACES Low

"Football is all very well as a game for rough girls, but is hardly suitable for delicate boys."
Oscar Wilde

I was now in Year 7 and technically in the under 11s age group, but for the new season I was moving up to the under 12s with Rovers. That meant we would be playing 11-a-side for the first time. Our double-winning squad had been reduced to just six players with the departure of goalkeeper Fran and defender Courtney, so we needed to attract a lot of new players. Fran's dad had had a disagreement with Richard and Russ about something so she had moved to another team. Courtney, however, just stopped playing altogether. That might sound odd, but the thing to remember is that there's no peer pressure in girls' football.

Unlike boys, who seem to live and breathe football, for a lot of girls who play the game it's just one of several pastimes. They might play for a while and then do something completely different before returning to football. It's not like you'll get left out in the playground if you don't play; in fact it's much more likely to be the other way round. I didn't hang around with any of my team-mates outside of football and none of my friends from school played, so when I was with my friends football was never discussed at all. If I'd packed it in I doubt any of them would have even noticed. Yet despite that, I still loved playing.

So after just a few weeks off, I was pleased that it was time to go again. Rovers were running trials to try and attract new players. Any girl in the area who was serious about football wanted to play for us, so when I turned up for trials there were lots of new players there and they were all really good. We ended up with a very strong squad of 15 players. I was sure we were going to have a brilliant team.

Also for the first time this year I was not the only McKevitt going for trials. Evan, who is two years younger than me, was also trying out for the first time. Mum was often working weekends, so Dad was relieved to find that the girls played on Saturday and the boys' matches were played on Sunday.

Evan had a trial with the under 9s at Ecclesall Rangers, which is one of the most successful boys' clubs in the city: all their teams play in the top two divisions. With Mum working I had no option but to go along and watch. Dad told me to put my boots on and said he'd ask the coach if I could join in: if not, we'd have our own kickabout.

As it happened, Evan's coach wasn't too keen on the idea of me joining in. My dad explained that I just wanted a game, but the coach said that, though he normally wouldn't have a problem, he was more concerned about what the parents would say about a non-trialist taking part. The guy standing next to him asked me how old I was. He said he was the manager of the under 12s team and I could train with them if I liked. I said 'yes, please' so he took me over to where the boys were training.

As we arrived I noticed that one of my laces was undone and bent down to tie it up.

"This is Niamh," the manager announced to the squad, "and she's going to be training with us today."

All the lads looked distinctly unimpressed. Then, as I was tying my laces, someone kicked the ball over to me. I instinctively rolled onto my back, lifted up my leg and kicked the ball straight back to him. It was a total fluke to be honest, as I'd just swung my leg at the ball without thinking I'd get anywhere near it. But I'd accidentally caught it perfectly and it was clear that they all thought I'd meant to do it.

"Oh my God!" I heard one of them say.

Evan's trial finished just before our training session was over. Dad had been watching him rather than me. Now they both came over to pick me up. Dad thanked the manager for letting me join in.

"No problem," he said, "we'll definitely take her."

"I'm sorry?" said Dad, sounding a bit confused.

"She had a super game and Niamh is exactly what we're looking for at centre-back. If you want to join there's a space for you in the squad."

I was very excited. This was a really good boys' team, so of course I wanted a place in the squad.

"That's a shame," said Dad. "I'm sure Niamh would love to play, but she's not allowed. The FA won't let girls play with boys beyond under 11s. I don't know why."

The manager looked disappointed, but not as disappointed as I felt.

"That's ridiculous," he said. "Anyone who'd watched that session would have seen that she's fine. I am really sorry. I'm sure Niamh would have done really well here."

I couldn't think of a good reason for banning girls from playing. Dad said he'd look into it for me and he discovered that the FA had consistently blocked any attempt to overturn the ruling. Several girls had spent years in the courts fighting it but had got nowhere.

Around this time there was a lot of coverage of the case of Alyshia Walker, a 13-year-old footballer from Scotland who played for a boys' team called Fauldhouse Foxes. In Scotland mixed football was allowed up to the age of 15. Alyshia was her team's star player, scoring 50 goals in 21 games, and she made history by becoming the first female to win the Scottish Youth FA Cup. As a result of that victory

Fauldhouse qualified for the UK Four Nations Finals of the Tesco Cup, but because the tournament was due to take place in Birmingham that year, the English FA banned her from playing.

There was a lot of support for Alyshia. David Little, secretary of the Scottish Youth FA said: "Personally I'm absolutely gutted by the whole thing. We are 100 per cent behind Alyshia and the club."

The secretary of the regional league, Iain Shaw, also said: "Two guys lost their jobs with *Sky Sports* for making sexist comments – is this any different? It's scandalous."

But the English FA refused to budge, although they did say that Alyshia could take part in the warm-up and the coin toss! You've got to wonder whether the person who came up with this idea was trying to make the situation better or worse.

By now I had started secondary school. In class, all the boys ever seemed to talk about was football: the teams they played for; how they'd got on at the weekend; who they were playing next week. I really wanted to join in. I tried a few times and although they weren't mean or anything, I could tell that they really weren't that interested. I think they found it quite difficult to relate to. Girls' football was just something they knew nothing about. They were, however, quite impressed to hear that I'd once been offered a place at Ecclesall Rangers, "They're a pretty good team. You must be half-decent."

Not long after the start of term, I had my trial at the Sheffield United CoE. It was scheduled for a Friday evening and was much more formal than any other trial I'd had before. It wasn't as much fun as Ecclesall Rangers. There were lots of forms to fill in and I had to get permission from the Rovers' club secretary (even though I technically wasn't even signed at that time).

The trial took place at Sheffield United's training ground, where both the boys' and girls' academies were based. This is a seriously impressive facility. At the time of writing, Sheffield United are only in League One but their academy has a reputation as one of the better ones in the country. There are treatment rooms, teaching rooms, gyms, a cafe and several grass and artificial pitches, including an indoor 11-a-side pitch.

The email said the evening was to begin with 'An introductory meeting with the Centre Head'. We arrived early and were given more forms to fill in and a 34-page rulebook to read. Dad filled in the forms while I read the rules. I was hoping it would explain what went on at the Centre of Excellence – what kind of training they did and who they played matches against, stuff like that. So I was a bit disappointed that it was just a long list of rules: things that academy players shouldn't or couldn't do; stuff about not wearing jewellery; not using a mobile phone; tying your hair up; what colour boots you could and couldn't wear; and what happened if you turned up late or forgot your kit or water bottle. The final rule on the last page was: 'Have Fun'.

Five women in Sheffield United CoE tracksuits arrived. The first introduced herself as the Centre Head.

"Hello trialists and parents and welcome to Sheffield United Girls' Centre of Excellence for your trial. Parents are not allowed to watch, so after this meeting trialists will be taken downstairs to be assessed by our coaches."

She looked at each of us.

"Now trialists, don't be nervous, but this will be coaching like you've never experienced before. It won't be like any football you've ever played before. It will be the most technical and challenging session you have ever experienced. You'll be exhausted at the end of it, and you may say, 'Mum and Dad that was the most incredible challenge for me,' but don't worry, when you're stepping up to elite level for the first time, it's completely normal for you to feel like that.

"You might ask why we're so keen to test you to the limits, and that's because this is one of the best academies in the country. Here at the Sheffield United Girls' Centre of Excellence we're only interested in one thing: England players. Don't let anyone tell you anything else. And unless you come to an accredited Centre of Excellence – like ours – you won't be able to play for England.

"It really is that simple. That's all we'll be thinking about when we assess you tonight: are these girls England players? Have they got the potential to be England players? Can we make them into England players? And that's why we need to get you in at this age. As it is, it'll take us at least two years to coach out all the bad habits you've picked up from grassroots football. If we get you when you're 13 it will be too late.

"Now then girls, be prepared for the most incredibly challenging experience of your lives. Don't worry if you don't understand what's going on, and don't think about why we've asked you to do something – just trust the coaches. They know what they're doing and what we're looking for. Is anyone nervous or daunted?"

I said I wasn't.

"Well, don't be! Just do your best. And remember to enjoy yourselves and have fun."

We were taken to join some girls who were already in the development squad. The training was actually quite good. The first part was all about fitness and I was pleased that I came first in most of the drills. At this time, I was doing athletics as well as football and specialised in racewalking. I became pretty good at it. I was British under 13s champion and represented Great Britain in the European Finals in Dublin. I gave up racewalking to concentrate on football, but all that training meant I built up lots of stamina, so I always found fitness drills easier than most.

Where I was weaker was on the drills that focused on my

first touch. To be honest, overall I thought the training was great, but I was familiar with almost all of the drills and it really wasn't unlike anything I'd done before. I didn't walk off the pitch exhausted either. I went back a couple more times and was eventually told by the coach that they'd like to offer me a place in the development squad. This would mean that I could stay with Rovers but receive proper coaching, which seemed the perfect outcome to me.

Middlewood Rovers only have three girls' teams but it is one of the biggest boys' clubs in the city. They have their own ground and most of their junior teams play in the top two divisions. One week, instead of training Richard arranged a pre-season friendly against our equivalent boys' team.

A lot of girls in our team had played mixed football and, like me, were really up for it, but quite a few parents voiced their reservations. Typically, the boys started out thinking it was going to be an easy run-out for them, but straight from the kick-off they realised they were actually in for a game.

At one point in the match a boy tried to go past Chanee, our defensive midfielder. Chanee looked more like Pixie Lott than Roy Keane, but looks can be deceiving and she took him out, winning the ball with a really hard sliding tackle. He didn't like that.

Chanee was a really good man-marker and Richard had told her to follow their central midfielder around and make sure he didn't get any time on the ball. She managed to do this really well. The match was tight and, as time went on, it became more and more physical. The boy Chanee was marking was clearly becoming more and more frustrated that she was tackling him every time he got the ball. And the fact that his own team's parents were taking the mickey out of him didn't help much either. After yet another challenge, he lost his temper and stamped on her.

You could tell right away that she was quite badly hurt

because she didn't move, and then it all kicked off. Parents ran on to the pitch – some to check that Chanee was okay, some to remonstrate with the boy who'd stamped on her. The game was abandoned.

Fortunately Chanee was not badly injured, but a few parents made it clear to Richard that they weren't at all happy about us playing against boys' teams, so that was the end of that and we never played against one again. I thought it was a bad foul, but it had nothing to do with the fact that we were a girls' team. Nobody would have felt the same way if the incident had taken place in a single sex game. I think the lad was just that kind of player: he's not the only one like that, I'm afraid. It is the sort of thing that people who think mixed football shouldn't be allowed will seize upon, but the fact is that it shouldn't happen at all, regardless of who is playing.

Over the next two years Rovers proved even more dominant than we had at under 11 level. At under 12 we won the league and cup again, only losing one match all season. At under 13 we won the league again, this time without dropping a point until the title was ours. Most matches were comfortable victories in which the defence was rarely involved, let alone tested. There were a few close games, but in most matches I had almost nothing to do. I was rarely stretched.

It felt like we were invincible. Everyone involved – the players, parents and coaches – thought we could win every game. And we did. However, this success was changing the atmosphere at the club. Some new players had been the stars at their previous teams, but at Rovers they were having to spend up to half the game on the bench. Training was getting worse as well. Russ was a good coach but I could see he was getting frustrated. Constantly winning had made some of the squad quite complacent: they had the impression that all we had to do was turn up, which, unfortunately, was true most of the time.

Within the team there were no major fallouts and everyone got on pretty well by and large, but you could see cliques emerging – people wanting to partner up with the same person for every training drill and play on the same team in practice matches. The situation deteriorated over time. Training with the CoE development squad meant I was getting two hours of good coaching every week, so it was less of an issue for me than some of the other players. However, it also made me think about playing football somewhere else.

The CoE development squad consisted of 16 players aged between 12 and 16. I was the youngest – in fact, the only 12-year-old. Most of the squad were two or three years older than me. It turned out that there weren't enough players for a development squad at each age group so we all trained together. As a consequence I was one of the weaker players. Some girls at 15 or 16 are practically fully grown. They were stronger than me, quicker than me, more comfortable on the ball than me and, in some cases, had been playing for twice as long as me. In other words, it was *exactly* the kind of challenge I was looking for.

There was no mucking about. It wasn't tolerated by the coaches but, more importantly, the players weren't there because we'd got a game on Saturday (the development squad didn't have a team and we never played matches) or wanted to hang out with their mates: they were there for two hours a week, every Friday night, because they wanted to get better at football. In some cases, they were travelling 20 or 30 miles to be there.

The two coaches, Pete and John, were in their 60s and had spent their entire careers coaching at professional football clubs. In fact, Pete was a UEFA A Licence coach, "Level 5 – the same as Alex Ferguson," he told me. They really knew how to handle a group. They were really funny too: like a comedy double-act in a lot of ways; always taking the mickey if you made a silly mistake, but really patient and willing to help if you needed it.

By making training fun they were able to really focus on the fundamentals of passing, control and movement, and help to improve our technique. It was really effective. I felt I was learning loads and soon other people started commenting on how much I was improving. It changed the way I played the game. For example, instead of diving in for challenges I tried to stay on my feet for as long as possible and position myself so that attackers would be forced to go where I wanted them to. I was more confident in possession too, which vastly improved my passing.

As time went on I realised that the development squad wasn't really a development squad at all, but more like a completely separate team. Nobody ever progressed from our squad to the CoE team and no coaches from the CoE ever came to watch the development squad train. In fact, I discovered that Pete and John were actually coaches from the boys' academy and were just paid to run our session independently. They had no other links to the girls' CoE at all. I once asked Pete how I could get into the proper CoE. He said he didn't know: "If it was down to me, I'd have the two squads playing regular matches against each other, but it's not. And no one ever asks us what we think about you lot as players. We just turn up and take the session."

I wasn't too bothered. I was enjoying the training and was still quite happy playing at Rovers.

One Friday evening in April however, it all changed. With the season drawing to a close we were each handed a letter at the end of training. It said that the FA was making changes to the structure of women's football. The current CoEs were being scrapped. They would be replaced by a smaller number (29) of new CoEs which would be much better funded. Sheffield United was going to be one of these 29 CoEs, but the bad news was that our development squad was going to be scrapped. In the future, development squads would become entirely separate Player Development Centres (PDCs). Unfortunately, there wasn't going to be one of those in our area for at least 12 months.

The letter finished by saying, 'We would like *all* of our development squad to attend trials for our new Centre of Excellence at the beginning of June.' I showed the letter to my dad

"That's a real shame," he said.

"It say's I can go for a trial at the Centre of Excellence, though," I replied.

"I think it's worth going along but I wouldn't read anything into that. It's what you might call 'a platitude': somebody saying something to be nice that they don't really mean. Look, you've been in the development squad for a year and no one from the Centre of Excellence has watched so much as a session. I think it's fair to assume that they're happy with who they've got and are not looking for anyone else. You might want to consider making alternative plans."

"Like what?" I said.

"This can't be the only Centre of Excellence there is so we could see if there's another nearby. Or perhaps there's a Player Development Centre in Leeds, near where I work. That might be a possibility. I'll have a look on the FA website in a few weeks' time. They'll probably have some information up by then."

Before the trials there was still an exciting tournament with Rovers. As league winners for the third time we were invited to take part in the ACES (All Cities Elite Shield) National Football Tournament held in Leicester. The ACES is the top grassroots competition in the country, open only to winners of the top division in the County leagues. The tournament was held over a weekend, with the boys competing on Saturday and girls on

Sunday. The league might have been a stroll this season, but the competition here was going to be much tougher.

We did really well in the tournament, losing on penalties in the semi-final, having been narrowly beaten in the group stages by the eventual winners, Blackpool, after our goalkeeper had to go off injured. It was a great experience.

During a break in the action I had gone with Dad to get some lunch. We got talking to a man sitting at our table and he turned out to be one of the organisers. He asked how I was enjoying the tournament. I said it was great to be playing so many competitive matches and Dad said he was really impressed with the quality of the football.

"That's really good to hear," said the organiser. "We introduced the girls' tournament a couple of years ago and this is the most entrants we've had. The boys' tournament is really well established and the standard is very high.

"Yesterday we had a team who were champions of Oxford. They'd not lost a game in five years, but got battered in every match 4-0, 5-0 and 8-0. They went home without even scoring a goal. I spoke to the coach afterwards. I was a bit worried he'd be upset, but he said he was really glad for the experience, as it had shut up some of the parents who thought their lads were destined for Man United. He said that it would probably make his job easier in the long run.

"One thing that is a bit disappointing, though. Yesterday, for the lads, we had 124 scouts attending from various academies, but today for the girls, we've not had a single one. We wrote to them all but they don't seem interested. It's a shame because there's a lot of talented players here."

It had been a really good experience, but when we got back to our league, Rovers would once again be winning most of their games easily. I had been starting to pin my hopes on getting a place at the CoE, but I was really worried that I wouldn't be good enough, or worse that Dad was right and they were just letting me try out to be kind.

Then with just a week to go before my trial, Dad came home from work and said he had some exciting news, "I think I've got the answer to all your problems. Forget about the Centre of Excellence – how would you like to play for a boys' team?"

Chapter 4
On Trial

"The FA is pleased that the resolution to amend its Rules to extend mixed football in the U13 age group received approval from The FA Shareholders at the AGM today (25 May). The resolution was fully supported by The FA Board, FA Executive and FA Council and the result means that girls and boys will be able to play in the same teams at U12 and U13 level from next season (2011/12)."

The Football Association, Statement on mixed football, 25th May 2011

The rule change took everyone by surprise. England had one of the lowest age limits for mixed football in the world, and that really hadn't looked like changing. Only the previous year – following a three-year study into mixed football, commissioned by the FA itself – a recommendation supported by its executive to extend the age limit had been dismissed out of hand at the shareholders' Annual General Meeting. In May 2011, following further consultation with UEFA, FIFA and a host of national associations, the FA finally caved in. As an under 13, I was just young enough to be able to take advantage.

I was so pleased. I was convinced that I would become a better player if I was playing boys' football. It wasn't really the Rovers team that was the problem, it was the standard of opposition. There were two other teams that could give us a game, but we'd won the league three years running and most of the matches were totally one-sided. There was usually very little defending to do and it could get a bit boring in games we were winning easily. I just wanted a bigger challenge.

However, there was one other problem to overcome before I could realise my goal: I needed to find a club. It was difficult to know where to start. Dad said he'd not watched any boys' under 13 football since he was 13 years old himself, so he didn't know what the standard would be like. In the end we came up with a starting point rather than a plan. I'd try out with a team in the middle of the range of divisions (there were seven in all) and see how that went.

Evan was playing at under 11 for a team called Hallam Rangers, and their under 13 team played in the E League (Division 5). That seemed a sensible place to start. Dad contacted the manager, Peter Dodsworth, and asked if I could come for a trial. Peter was very helpful. He said I was welcome to come to the next training session, but explained that Hallam wasn't really a team that ran trials and unless he lost a player to another club he wasn't really looking to sign anyone, boy or girl, no matter how good they were. Dad said that it was as much for us to find out about whether boys' football was for me at all than anything else. Peter said I should come down and, on the basis of how well I did, he'd be happy to recommend some other clubs at a level to suit my playing ability.

I knew it wasn't really a trial, but I got more and more nervous as the day approached. I was worried that the boys would be so much better than me and that I'd look stupid, but my dad said he was sure I'd do okay.

Hallam train on a huge field at the top of Lodge Moor; one of the highest hills in Sheffield. Their ground has the reputation for being the coldest in the league. When we turned up we could see the under 13s already training in the distance. It was a really long walk over to them. I had butterflies in my stomach. A few of them noticed me.

'Look a new player coming to try out.'

A bit closer...

'He looks a bit like a girl.'

A bit closer...

'He looks a lot like a girl.'

Almost there...

'It is a girl! Is this some kind of a joke?'

Peter came to meet us. He was very friendly.

"Hi Niamh, I've been really looking forward to meeting you."

He turned to the players.

"Lads, Niamh is here to play with us tonight. Niamh, why don't you go and join in with the boys and get yourself warmed up?"

The lads looked genuinely shocked. A few of them may have played against the odd girl at under 9 or under 10, but that would have been quite a few years ago. I was guessing that none of them had been keeping up to speed with the FA's policy on mixed gender football. It was a reaction I was to get used to over the next few years and I quickly came to actually enjoy it, but today it just made me feel more nervous.

The session started with four laps of the pitch to test our fitness, followed by a few dribbling and possession drills. It's very difficult in these kind of exercises to work out who's a good player or not, but I got the feeling that I was doing well. I was the first to finish the laps (thank you athletics!) and completed the drills without too many problems. This filled me with confidence as we moved into a practice match.

Peter split us into two teams and played me at right-back, which was an unfamiliar position at the time. This put me up against the left-winger, a kid called Benjamin who had been the previous season's top scorer. Much to my surprise I found the game very comfortable. The boys were all decent players, but nowhere near as good as I'd imagined. Benjamin was the best of the lot, but I made sure he didn't get past me. I grew in confidence and started calling for the ball and shouting to the other members of my team. If this was boys' football then I knew I could definitely cope with it.

Even before the end of training I could see Peter deep in conversation with my dad on the touchline. I hoped he was saying something positive.

"I was just saying to your dad here, I'm really impressed – you're definitely a player. I'd love to sign you if I could, but unless someone decides to leave we always stick with the same set of lads. Things might change but at the moment everybody is telling me that they're staying, so I haven't got a space. I'm sorry."

"Are there any other clubs you could recommend?" asked Dad.

"I have been thinking about that. To be honest, the problem I think you'll have is that you can only play for a year. I think quite a few coaches will be put off by that. But in terms of ability, I think you could look a couple of divisions above us, say, in the D or the C League.

"There's a team not too far from you called Abbey Lane. They're in the D League. They hammered us in the cup and play a really good passing game. Very impressive: reminded me of Arsenal. I think they only just missed out on promotion last season so they might well be looking to strengthen the squad. Niamh is definitely good enough."

At home we had a look at the previous season's league tables and we decided to contact three teams, just in case. I liked the sound of Abbey Lane the most. They were in the D League and had indeed just missed out on promotion, so we decided to give them a go. We also found another team not too far away called Sheffield Rangers, who had been relegated to the C League. Dad reckoned they would probably have lost one or two players and might well have places. Finally, there was the local team, Millhouses Boys. This was a long shot as they had won promotion to the B League, but given that they played their home matches within walking distance from our house, we just thought that a trial at that level would be good experience and it was easy to get to.

This seemed like a good plan: teams in the second, third and fourth division. Hopefully one of them would want me. The next stage was to try and get a trial. Dad emailed the three coaches to see if they were looking for players. He was very careful with the wording.

Hello,

I wondered if you're looking for any new players for the under 13s next season?
My eldest is looking for a club. Niamh is a good player and has spent the last 12 months in the development squad at the Sheffield United Academy. Niamh is a centre-back; a physical player who reads the game well.

Please let me know if you're interested in having a look.

Best regards

Steve

"If they've got places, that should spark some interest," said Dad. "The fact that you're a girl is irrelevant, so I've not mentioned it."

He smiled and added, "And of course everyone knows that Niamh's a girl's name, so there should be no confusion at all."

Mum's family is Irish and my brother, sister and me have Irish – or Gaelic – names. There's no 'v' in the Gaelic alphabet so they use 'mh' instead. My name is pronounced 'Neve' (rhymes with Steve) or 'Nee-ave' if you're from Ulster. It's quite a common name in Ireland: not so popular, it turns out, in South Yorkshire. A lot of people struggle with it. I get called 'Naymar', 'Niammer', 'Nymph' and – most of all – 'Neme', even by people who know me quite well. My friend's mum had no problem until she saw it written down. Now she just tries to avoid saying my name at all. And if she has to, she just mumbles the ending. Still I suppose it could be worse. My sister is called Aoife (pronounced 'Ee-fer' as in 'E for' elephant). I think it actually works better if you spell it backwards.

Our plan worked, but it was no surprise when Steve, the manager of Abbey Lane, wrote back to us the same evening saying, "Yes, we are having trials. They start this Thursday at 6:30 and your lad Niall is very welcome to join us. I won't be there, but I've passed your details on to Martin my assistant and he's looking forward to seeing you both."

Wrong name and gender, but at least he got the right nationality.

Chris, the manager of Sheffield Rangers, phoned Dad and offered me a trial the following Wednesday. Once they'd had a bit of a chat, he said he had no problems trialling a girl. He'd lost a lot of players and was looking at bringing in at least five and possibly six, so trials would continue for three weeks. We didn't hear anything back from Millhouses, but I was trying out at two different clubs, which would hopefully be enough.

It was a beautiful summer's evening when we arrived at the school playing fields where Abbey Lane were training. A man in a white T-shirt and shorts was putting cones out while a group of lads were having a kickabout with varying degrees of enthusiasm. They were pretending not to notice the girl in the football kit speaking to their coach, but out of the corner of my eye I noticed that the pace of their game had slowed somewhat.

"Hello, you must be Martin," said Dad. "This is Niamh."

"Niamh?" said Martin, looking confused. "Steve told me to expect a Niall, but he didn't say anything about a Niamh. You do realise this is a lads' team?"

Dad said it wasn't a mistake and explained about the rule change.

"Just have a look at her. I don't think it'll be a waste of your time."

Martin nodded.

"Fine by me then. Go over and join the lads and we'll see what you've got."

The lads were less than 20m away, but it was one of the longest walks of my life. They looked really cocky. I could feel my heart starting to pound and my mouth suddenly felt very dry. I took a sip of water in what I hoped was an equally cool way, but the effect was spoiled slightly when I spilt some down my front. No one was nasty, but no one greeted me or, in fact, said anything at all.

There was a distinct avoidance of eye contact. The kickabout had evolved slightly into a sort of game in which one player – who clearly fancied himself as the most skilful and was, I assumed, a winger – took on each of the others in turn and dazzled them with a selection of dummies and step-overs. To be fair he was pretty good at them. He had quick feet and was showing the ball with his right, inviting his opponent to make a challenge then dragging it back with his left at the last second. The more people he beat the cockier he became.

As he was working his way round to me, I noticed that he always dragged the ball back with his left foot. Most players are right footed, so he was able to anticipate where the challenge was coming from. When it came to my turn, I went in with my left instead of my right, gambling on where he was going to drag the ball to rather than where it was. I made a perfect tackle and took him completely by surprise. Not only did I win the ball, but the challenge caught him off balance and he fell down rather heavily. There was a brief pause before the rest of the team started killing themselves laughing. The sound confirmed his worst fears: yes, he really had just lost the ball to a girl! The ice was broken and one of the boys asked me who I used to play for. I had made that all-important first impression.

It was a good start to the trial, but things went even better from there. No offence, but you could tell Abbey Lane were a better side than Hallam Rangers. They had some really good players and made fewer mistakes in the drills. I was getting a lot of well dones from Martin, which was a good sign. During the practice match I was played in central defence with a kid called Josh. He said he'd been for a trial with Brunsmere, who played in the A League, but had missed out and was now spending another season at Abbey Lane. I felt comfortable playing alongside Josh and we immediately developed a good understanding. He was very vocal, so we never went for the same ball or marked the same man.

It's not always the case, but I could tell I was having a good game. I seemed to be winning my headers and tackles, and my passes were finding team-mates rather than opponents. It just felt right and I decided there and then that I really wanted to play for Abbey Lane.

At the end of the session I no longer felt like an outsider. I'd learned a few names – Sam, Dex, Josh and Jordan (the guy I'd put on his backside and the previous season's top scorer). Judging from the shouts during the practice match a few people had also learned mine. Not everyone there was a good player. There were a few I was a bit unsure about, but I thought overall we had the makings of a very good team. Most importantly though, Martin was impressed.

"You played well, Niamh. We're short of a centre-back and you look like exactly the kind of player we need. Steve's back next week, so in the meantime I'll let him know exactly what I think and you just come along again. If it was up to me I'd sign you tonight, but I'm only the assistant manager unfortunately. I can't see there being any problems though."

Dad also thought I'd played well. He said the other parents were sceptical initially, but had quite quickly become enthusiastic.

I'd really enjoyed myself and had pretty much made up my mind that I was going to play for Abbey Lane no matter what happened at Sheffield Rangers, even though they were in the higher division. The Sheffield Rangers trial had a very different feel to the one at Abbey Lane. I had been worried that all the boys would be better than me, but I now knew that that was not the case. Chris, the manager, seemed like a really decent guy. He didn't bat an eyelid when I turned up and seemed to know what he was talking about. The problem was that, with so many players leaving, he'd advertised for new squad members and 24 boys (and a girl) had turned up. A few groups of two or three mates had come along, but most of us had come on our own. I wasn't intimidated at all this time: I was more interested in seeing how the players here compared with Abbey Lane. Despite playing in a higher division, there were fewer outstanding players and several trialists didn't really look good enough. It was hard to work out who was going to be in the team and I just couldn't picture myself playing there.

Chris said I was welcome to come back the following week, when he'd be whittling down the numbers, but at the moment he had very little idea who was going to be in the squad. He was starting from scratch. I had wanted to join a team with a few spaces, but this felt like there were too many gaps to fill and not enough good players to fill them.

It had only been a fortnight, but the idea of going back to play with girls was already starting to feel a bit strange.

I think the biggest difference is in mindset rather than ability. Girls are less inclined to show off their skills than boys, probably because they know the other girls wouldn't be impressed. If you tell a group of girls 'This is a practice match', they will think of it as exactly that: an opportunity to practise; something that's not important, which will be forgotten about in the morning. Tell a group of boys 'This is a practice match' and they'll treat it as an opportunity to show off/settle scores/skill everyone/tackle their best mates as hard as possible or score 10 goals. Over the years I've experienced training matches played with the same intensity as a derby and seen proper fights break out between boys who were the best of mates five minutes earlier. I've never seen that happen in a girls' game.

The second trial at Abbey Lane went even better than the first. I was getting to know the players and feeling much more confident. I won the heading drill and played well in the game. I was getting a lot of praise from the coaches. And again, I was feeling that I could build a good partnership in central defence with Josh. We did set-piece drills – corners and free kicks. There was one guy who obviously fancied himself – not in the same way as Jordan with 'the skills to pay the bills' – but he obviously thought he was going to get his head on everything. He decided to mark me, no doubt thinking it would be easier, but I was pushing him all over the pitch and he didn't get near the ball once. There was a lot of mickey-taking from his team-mates.

This week, Steve the manager was there. He seemed okay but he wasn't as immediately friendly as Martin. He took the defenders for a heading drill. I felt pretty confident. All those weekends of having the ball blasted at me in the park by Dad had paid off: no way was this guy going to be chucking the ball at me that hard. I felt I nailed it. I was winning more than anyone else. I was hopeful that Steve would offer me a place in the team, but the conversation we had at the end was a little bit odd.

Steve seemed really impressed – he even said that I was 'a great player' – and then went on to really try to sell the club to me. He explained that they'd just missed out on promotion last season and were really keen to kick on this year.

"The number of points we got would have seen us promoted from every other division in the league. We want to make sure we do it this year," he said.

He talked about how good the pitches were, what training was like and what he thought I would learn from it. He said that I'd probably be playing in the centre of defence with Josh and, as he liked to play a passing game, was pleased to see that the way I played would suit them well.

It sounded like he was trying to persuade me to come, but that was all a bit unnecessary. I'd already decided. I said it sounded great and that I'd love to join the team. I expected him to say something like, 'Then welcome aboard' or 'Good to have you, Niall' but instead he said, "Come back next Thursday then and we'll have another look."

I was a bit disappointed, but Dad told me not to worry. If I played like I had the past two weeks I'd be fine and, given how hard Steve had tried to sell the club to me, it seemed obvious he wanted me.

The following week Dad was working, so Mum had to take me to the third trial. But by now it no longer felt like a trial. For a start, apart from me there were no other trialists. There had been a couple of other lads trying out the last couple of weeks, but they weren't there that evening. I guessed they'd been told they hadn't made the cut. I was getting on with the lads quite well. Having got over their initial shock they were now treating me like one of the team: calling my name when they wanted a pass, or putting my name on it when they played it to me, or telling me to get tight or drop off. All basic stuff really, but it showed that they were taking me seriously. They were looking to include me rather than shut me out: they wouldn't have done that if they didn't think I was any good.

After the opening drills we were split into attack and defence again. This week the defenders worked with Martin. I played at centre-back again and afterwards Martin said he was pleased to see we were all developing a really good understanding together and thought we were going to have a really good season.

At the end Steve called everyone's parents over and handed out registration forms. He said to Mum: "Thanks very much for bringing Niamh. She's a great player and I think she'll go really far in the women's game."

"Thanks," I said.

"But unfortunately, I'm not going to sign her. I've already got a player in that position."

I couldn't believe what I'd just heard. Mum said that it was a surprise as we thought the trial was going well.

"No it has," said Steve. "As I said I'm really impressed, but I've already got a lad playing in that position, so sorry it's a no I'm afraid."

I was absolutely devastated. I just wanted to get away as quickly as possible. I was glad that Mum was with me because she just said, "Okay then", smiled politely and we left. 'What had been point of inviting me back three times?' I thought. Mum agreed that it did seem rather an odd thing to do. Dad was a little less diplomatic.

"Surely he must have known that when we contacted him a month ago? Why did he feel the need to drag you back three times? What a complete waste of everyone's time," he said when we told him (only with a lot more swearing).

Dad was right about the waste of time. We were now three weeks into June trials and a lot of teams would now – like Abbey Lane – have their squads sorted. I was really worried I wouldn't find a club anywhere.

"Don't panic," said Dad. "There are 75 other teams out there and I'm sure you'll find one. It'll just mean travelling a little bit further, that's all. We'll have a look now and send a few more emails out."

We spent about an hour going through the leagues and found three teams in Sheffield who were all advertising for defenders: two from League E and one from League F. I was disappointed to be playing so far down the divisions, as I felt sure I had the ability to play higher up but it didn't seem like I'd get the chance to prove it. We decided not to waste any more time and Dad set about contacting the managers right away. He opened his laptop to send out some more emails.

You have 1 New Message

From: Iain Lothian
Subject: Re: Under 13s Trials

Dear Steve,

Sincere apologies for the delay in responding, but for some reason your email went straight to my spam folder and I've only picked it up this evening. If your lad is still looking for a club we'd be very interested in taking a look at him. We've been running trials for three weeks but are desperate for another defender and no one we've seen so far has been good enough.

If you can make it, we've got a final trial tomorrow evening at 6pm. I appreciate you might be already sorted and we're quite late in the day, but as I say, we are desperate, so I will promise that I can give you a definitive yes or no tomorrow night.

Best regards
Iain
U13 Manager
Millhouses Boys JFC

Chapter 5
One Last Chance

"Women should be in the discotheque, the boutique and the kitchen, but not in football."
Ron Atkinson

This time I wasn't nervous: I was determined. We had contacted Millhouses at the time because we thought it would be a good experience; a one-off or a bonus while I settled happily for a club in a lower division. Now it seemed like my last chance. Everybody told me to just do my best. Except Dad. He said that that might not be enough and I should have a plan as well. He told me to work out who their best striker was and put myself up against him. If I could show I could cope with him, then that would hopefully give them the confidence to pick me.

Dad asked Peter at Hallam Rangers if he knew anything about Millhouses.

"They've gone right the way up the leagues. Promoted four seasons running. We played them a couple of years ago. Very nice set up. Iain, the coach, is a good guy and they had one kid up front who was like Usain Bolt. He could probably have won the game on his own," he said.

Finding out who Millhouses' best player was turned out to be easy. I asked Louis and Chris, a couple of guys who played in the school team, if they knew Millhouses. They both said, "Oh my God! You'll be playing with Bilal."

Even I knew who Bilal was. He's one of those kids everyone who played football seemed to know. There were rumours that he was actually 18 and had a false passport; that he had been seen driving a car; that he was shaving at 10 and had a moustache and beard. I was certain that none of this was true, but Bilal had just scored 47 goals in 22 games – more than anyone else in the entire league – so I had no doubt that he was a very good striker.

I had actually come across Bilal once before. When I was at primary school, we competed in an inter-school Sportshall Athletics event, which is a smaller, indoor version of real athletics. There was one kid from another school who looked like one of the teachers. No one wanted to compete against him and he won everything. That was Bilal.

One of Mum's friends, Shirley, had a son called Alex who played for Millhouses. He was team captain and had spent a few years in the development squad at the Sheffield United Academy. I knew he was a very good player. Shirley said that Bilal and his brother, Sheriyar (who also played for the team), lived across the road from where Millhouses used to train. They'd have their own kickabout on the same field and were always pestering Iain to let them join in. Finally he relented one week and allowed them to play in a practice match at the end. They were so good that he signed them both up immediately.

Iain welcomed me and seemed like a really decent guy. Dad had told him ahead of the trial that I was a girl but he said he didn't care what 'gender, race or species' players were as long as they could play football. After the usual introductions Iain asked me to join the rest of the players. Given the legend, I was a bit disappointed when I saw Bilal for the first time since primary school. Millhouses were a pretty tall team, but disappointingly, although he looked very strong, Bilal turned out to be closer to normal rather than superhuman size. There were three or four lads taller than him.

If that was reassuring then the rest of what was going on in the kickabout wasn't. It was clear that all these boys were very good at football. It wasn't just one really good kid skilling everyone else and showing off, they were all doing tricks with the ball and trying to 'do' each other. The biggest guy, Dan, who turned out to be one of the centre-backs, was doing stepovers and drag-backs and taking 'rabonas' from outside the box. 'And he's just a centre-back,' I thought. A striker called Munib looked like a dancer when he ran with the ball. He was just so skilful, you never knew what he was going to do next. Bilal wasn't joining in at all. He was standing about chatting to a couple of the others.

Iain had known that I was a girl, but I didn't know if he'd told his players or not. No one was particularly friendly or unfriendly. They were quite surprised to see me arrive, but were playing it cool. Their reaction when I was introduced was entirely neutral.

The session began well for me. I came second in a fitness test and was only beaten by Munib, who was the South Yorkshire cross-country champion. But then we moved on to sprint training and I was near the back – though not last, thankfully. I couldn't help noticing just how quick some of the players were. Bilal was frighteningly fast, but his brother Sheriyar, Dan, Alex, Munib and a midfielder called Chris weren't far behind. That was the first time I'd seen something that you wouldn't find in the girls' game. I'm pretty quick. I've competed at County level over 200m and I've played with and against some really fast girls, but that explosive acceleration – the blistering pace from a standing start over five yards that you see, at its peak, in players at the top level like Theo Walcott or Lionel Messi – is something that I've only really come across in the boys' game.

The first drill we did was 'Numbers', which is one of my favourites. Players are split into two teams and each one is given a number that pairs them with a member of the opposing group. The coach rolls the ball into the centre and calls out a number. If your number is called, you've got to sprint round a cone and onto the pitch and compete in a one v one until either someone scores or the ball goes out of play. Numbers is a game based around skill and these were by far the most skilful players I'd ever played with. If I gave the lad I was up against any time at all, he would run rings round me.

Unfortunately, I hadn't been concentrating when Iain gave us our numbers – there were too many distractions. After a few rounds, Iain called out "Five." Nobody on my team moved, so I realised that it must be me. My slow reaction didn't go unnoticed and, as I set off, I heard a couple of the boys in my group groan and one mutter, "Oh, for God's sake!"

I sprinted as fast as I could, but I had some ground to make up. I could see that I was up against Sheriyar. He wasn't running flat out though (I'm almost certain that was because he was up against me). As I turned round the cone it was obvious that we were going to get to the ball at exactly the same time. This meant that we'd be competing for a 50/50 ball. The player who wins a 50/50 is almost always the one who wants it the most; the one who goes in hardest. And at that moment in time, I wanted it much more than Sheriyar!

I steamed into the tackle as hard as I could. Bang! We both made contact... and I came out with the ball. Sheriyar was on his backside so I rolled it into the empty net. All I could hear was the sound of boys laughing, but it wasn't at me.

"Sherry man, you just got done by a girl! She's proper smashed you, bro!"

I turned round and saw that Sheriyar was laughing too, holding a hand up as if to say, 'You did me' and acting as if he was taking the applause.

"Nice one, Niamh," said Iain.

I think he was quite pleased.

We moved on to the practice match, which also went well. People were calling my name and I was seeing a lot of the ball. I felt like I was giving a good account of myself. I was up against Bilal. He might not have been that big, but he was the strongest player I'd ever played against. The first time we faced each other one-on-one I gave him too much space. He beat me and scored. It all happened so quickly: one second he was in front of me and I seemed to have him under control, the next he was putting the ball in the back of the net. After that I got much tighter. The second time I got the challenge in early and the third I slid in and won the ball. For the second time that night, the boys were laughing because I'd tackled someone.

"Hey man – chill out. It's just training!" Bilal said.

I took that as a good sign.

At the end of the trial Iain was polite. He said it went well, but he also said he needed to talk with Dave, the assistant coach, before any decisions were made. After last week's disappointment I didn't want to get my hopes up.

It was a couple of hours later when Dad got the call. I'd made it – Millhouses wanted me to join the squad. The bitter disappointment of Abbey Lane was gone in an instant. Thanks to them, I was now going to be playing in the B League. I'd won leagues and cups in the past, but this felt like my biggest achievement. Yet I was more relieved than happy, and I couldn't wait to get started.

Chapter 6
Playing with Boys

"Every single day I wake up and commit myself to becoming a better player."
Mia Hamm, former US footballer. The first player ever, male or female, to score over 150 international goals

The final squad at Millhouses was a very interesting mix: 14 players, 12 different nationalities and two genders. I was effectively joining a brand new team. Despite being promoted, Iain and Dave had decided that the previous season's squad would be unable to compete in the higher league so they had been actively seeking new players.

As well as myself, five new lads had joined. Three had dropped down from the A League. Chris, a centre-midfielder, and Dan, a centre-back, had both joined from Sheffield United Junior Blades. Guido, a boy from my school who had also played basketball for England, was our goalkeeper. Another midfielder, Zak, had joined from the division below, which made me pleased to know I was not going to be the only one stepping up.

However, the most eye-catching signing was Munib, a right-winger and the most skilful player I'd ever seen. Yet other than down the park with his mates, Munib had never played before. This was his first proper team. I hated going up against Munib in training more than anyone else. His feet were so quick that you could never get the ball off him. He'd always try to tempt you into putting in a tackle, but if you were stupid enough to do that, he'd just whip the ball away and was gone. Dad said the best thing to do against him was not to put in a tackle at all, but to stand up and try and push him out wide. But even doing that was much harder than it sounds.

Iain said he was very excited about the squad and what we could achieve. In order to bed in the new signings he arranged some friendlies before we broke up for the summer holidays. Our first was against a team called Porter. I was really pleased when I heard this, as Porter were another local club and most of the boys from my old primary school team played for them. It felt like a really good place to begin my time in boys football. Not only would I know quite a few boys on the other side – which was a bit of a relief for my first match – but in a way, I'd also get the chance to play against the school team I was considered not good enough to join a few years earlier.

Porter were in the same league as Hallam Rangers and had finished the previous season just one place above them. I'd have happily signed for Hallam a few weeks ago, so this would also be a good chance for me to see how much difference there was across the leagues.

We arrived at the ground and I could see a few Millhouses players warming up in the far goal, which meant I had to walk past the Porter players to get to them. They were surprised to see me and a few of them were whispering and laughing, more out of disbelief than anything else. However, this time I didn't feel intimidated at all. I said 'hello' to all the lads I knew from school. I wasn't on my own any more. I was here with my team – a very good team – and I quite liked the fact the other side weren't taking me seriously. I knew that they soon would be.

Iain announced the starting line-up and said he was going to try me at left-back. I was a bit surprised because I'd never played full-back before and I'm right footed. Iain said not to worry, as he just wanted to try a few things out.

The match got underway and we were immediately on top. I felt really confident. Dan was alongside me at centre-back and he was constantly shouting instructions. In fact, I noticed there was generally a lot more shouting going on compared to the girls' matches. Everyone was very keen to get on the ball. The Porter right-winger wasn't giving me any problems and there was always a pass or two on. I kept it simple, either playing it inside to Chris and Alex or down the line to Luke. Up front, Munib and Bilal were running riot. Neither of them liked passing, but the way they were running at the defenders was certainly proving effective. I played for an hour of the 70 minutes, and by the time I came off we were winning 9-0.

Porter scored two late goals to make the final score 9-2, but I was actually quite pleased about the fact that we'd conceded those goals while I'd been off the pitch. Dave, the assistant coach, said I'd done really well and that they didn't do man of the match – "player of the game!" Iain corrected him – but if they had done, I'd have got it.

Dad was enthusiastic after the game.

"I've watched an awful lot of football, but that looks like one hell of a team you've joined there," he said. "It is really going to bring you on playing with those lads. I'm looking forward to seeing how well the team does. I can honestly say I was impressed by every single player."

He also said that rather than worry about playing left-back I should concentrate on making the position my own.

Going into school the next day was the first time I'd ever really been able to join in with the football banter. Dan, Porter's captain, sat in front of me for science. I liked Dan and got on well with him, but this was too good an opportunity to miss.

"Morning Dan," I said. "Didn't you have a game last night?"

"Just shut up, Niamh!" he said.

"What, don't you remember Dan? Was it 9-0?"

"9-2 actually!"

"See you do remember. So you'll also know that is was actually 9-0 until I went off, wasn't it?"

"Yeah, but I still scored"

"Only when I wasn't on the pitch, Dan."

I could see why the boys like to take the mickey out of each other so much. I suppose you can write off a 3-0 defeat, but it's much more difficult to concede nine and claim you were unlucky. Dan is known to be a good player, so earning bragging rights because of our win made me feel that I'd finally been accepted. 'This is it, I'm finally on the inside,' I thought.

The next match made me think that the coming season would be a breeze. It was against an older side, Millhouses Under 14s. We beat them 7-0.

'We're brilliant!' I thought. Practically unbeatable, because we'd just hammered two teams. 'This is simple. It's going to be easy.'

As it turned out, though, my overconfidence was somewhat short-lived. Five days later we played Sheffield Sixes.

Sheffield Sixes were the boys' team Rovers had beaten 2-0 three years earlier. That must have been their low point because they were now playing in the A League. There was a big gap in girls' football between the first and second division, but I had expected that, with so many more teams in boys' football, the gap between each division would be much less pronounced. In fact there was something of a step-up between every division, but the higher up you went the bigger the step, and the greatest of all was between the top two leagues. Sixes had just been promoted as champions of the B League and their best player, Frank, had scored 29 goals from midfield.

Something I'd noticed about Millhouses was that very few parents turned up to watch. Apart from Dad and the coaches, there were usually just four or five spectators. So coupled with the fact that this was just a pre-season friendly, the first thing that surprised me was just how many people were here to watch. The reason soon became clear: they were all here to see Frank.

As we walked from the car park to the pitch, Dad bumped into somebody he knew who also turned out to be coming to watch the game. He was wearing a Sheffield United jacket and I assumed that he was a parent of one of the boys who played for Sheffield Sixes, but as they started talking I realised he actually worked for United.

His name was Mark and he was the club's chief scout. He was very friendly and told Dad he had come here with some of his colleagues because they were about to sign Frank. This was actually going to be Frank's last ever game for Sheffield Sixes. Mark said they also wanted to look at Chris from our team.

"You've joined a decent side," said Mark. "We've had a look at quite a few of your lads. Alex was with us for a couple of years, and we had Bilal on a six-week trial last season."

Clubs are rarely happy to see their best players called up to an academy. Sixes didn't want to lose Frank and we didn't want to lose Chris either. Perhaps with that in mind, Mark had brought along one of the boys from his development squad as a potential replacement.

But it wasn't only Sheffield United who were represented, as Sheffield Wednesday and Barnsley also had scouts at the match. This was a completely new experience for me. I'd been playing for arguably one of the best grassroots girls' teams in the country in cup finals and national tournaments, but I'd never seen a scout at any game. In fact, I was pretty sure they didn't exist in women's football. Yet here I was in my third match – just a pre-season friendly – and the touchline was crawling with them.

Frank was easy to pick out during the warm-up. He might have only been 12, but he was the only one who looked fully grown. And not fully grown into a normal-sized adult like Bilal either, but fully grown into the Incredible Hulk! We had some big players – our centre-backs, Dan and Sheriyar, were maybe as tall as Frank, and in midfield Luke and Finlay were not far behind – but they all still looked like boys while Frank looked like a man. He could probably have pushed all four of them over at the same time.

On top of the 'Frank Factor' was Sixes' apparently well-earned reputation for being 'a bit aggressive'. Together this made for a much less confident pre-match atmosphere than the previous two games. You could sense there was some fear within the squad. So when Iain told us the team, I did actually think, 'Oh God, I'm starting!' I'm sure I wasn't alone.

It was the most physical game I'd ever played in. Player for player, Sixes weren't better than us, but they seemed to win every 50/50 ball. The tackles were flying in. In centre-midfield, Chris and Alex couldn't really get going and when we got the ball out to Munib or Bilal, they didn't have time to get the ball down before the opposition defenders smashed into them. I was in a state of shock for the first few minutes, trying to keep out of trouble – which is a bit difficult when you're in defence and your team is getting battered. I'd never played in a game like this before.

In the middle of it all was Frank. Every time he got on the ball, it looked like Sixes were going to score. And he got on the ball a lot. It wasn't just his size or his skill, it wasn't even the fact that he had brilliant touch and technique and was lightning quick, it was the effect that he had on the players around him. Frank seemed to inspire and energise the lads on his own team. They were always looking to pass to him. He'd run at our midfield playing a series of one-twos and was so quick it was impossible for them to track him. That meant that the centre-backs had to commit themselves to a tackle. I was so glad I wasn't playing centre-back.

The one player on our team who didn't seem remotely scared at all was Dan. I really liked Dan, but his position as 'Team Enforcer' was well earned. I've learned that every team needs a player like Dan: someone who's fearless, or foolhardy enough not to be intimidated. He gave me the confidence to get stuck in, and rather than hiding I started looking to get involved.

Once I did that I really began to enjoy it. The pace was ferocious, but it was really exhilarating. Dan's commitment wasn't always enough though, and our busiest player was Guido, who had a fantastic half diving in at people's feet and pulling off a string of great saves. Between them, Guido and Dan were largely responsible for us only being 3-0 down at half time.

In the half-time team talk Iain was very clear. He told us that this was the standard we had to get to.

"This is the kind of team you'll be playing every week, not Porter. You've got to rise to the challenge and stop being scared, otherwise you'll get murdered every time."

They made some substitutions for the second half. I wasn't taken off and this time my reaction was completely different: 'Great, I'm staying on!'

The other thing that happened was that Sheriyar took out their star player. Frank went through for the umpteenth time, but over-hit the ball slightly and Sheriyar slid in and took out the man and the ball. It was a hard tackle, but fair. The ref signalled for a throw-in. Frank stayed down and ended up being carried off for treatment. We were all taking the mickey out of Sheriyar.

"God Sherry, you've killed Frank! You'd better hope he doesn't come back on or you'll be dead too."

We all laughed (well, all except Sheriyar when Frank did come back on), but his tackle did make a difference and people who'd been missing in action started getting involved. Our hard work paid off and we pulled two goals back to finish with a respectable and confidence building 3-2 defeat.

I learned more in that game than any other I'd played in before. Dad said I probably wouldn't be coming up against anyone as good as Frank anytime soon, but otherwise it was going to be like that every week.

It was exactly the kind of experience I'd been looking for: testing myself against the best players and teams. If I was going to get better then this was the way to do it. I knew it would be a steep learning curve and I knew it wasn't going to be easy, but I now felt that I was ready for it.

Chapter 7

Changing Rooms and Changing Rules

"Somebody better get down there and explain offside to her... The game's gone mad. Did you hear charming Karren Brady this morning complaining about sexism? Do me a favour, love."

Richard Keys, former *Sky Sports* presenter, talking about Sian Massey, a female linesman, before a Premier League match in 2011

I felt so lucky to have been able to take advantage of the mixed football rule change. The rule change was driven through by the FA's Women's Football Development Officer, Rachel Pavlou. It was a change that the FA had resisted for years, and without Rachel it might not have happened at all.

In July 2006, the year before I began playing, a committee of MPs urged the FA to change its rules and allow mixed teams beyond the age of 11. Women's football was growing rapidly: the number of teams had grown from 80 in 1993 to 8,000 in 2005 and there were 130,000 registered players. Their report also argued that the FA: "Should take a lead in removing the cultural and practical barriers which undermine the women's game... [the rule is] an artificial barrier to girls' potential development – and a possible deterrent to more females taking up the sport."

The FA responded by asking Rachel Pavlou to commission a study. A team from Brunel University, headed by Dr Laura

Hills, was asked to identify the key issues involved in mixed-gender football and their research took three years to complete. In the 2007/08 season a number of mixed-gender trials took place at under 12, under 13 and under 14 levels, but the FA wasn't satisfied with the data so the trials were extended to the 2008/09 and 2009/10 seasons.

Dr Hills' report was finally completed in January 2009. Her research showed that girls would benefit from playing with boys due to the opportunities for skill development, challenge and enjoyment, and that boys and girls would benefit socially from the friendships they develop and gain respect for each other as team-mates. In terms of child development and physiology, there was a 'considerable overlap between boys and girls in relation to size, motor skill development and ability between the ages of 11 and 13'. Dr Hills recommended that the FA should allow girls to play with boys up to an older age group.

This still wasn't enough for the FA, who spent a further year carrying out an independent risk assessment. A company called Logistique was appointed to assess the risk of injuries to players. A year later they reported that no girl participating in any mixed-gender team studied had required any treatment for injuries.

In March 2010, the FA finally announced that its research was complete and that: "Subject to formal approval at the FA's AGM in May, [the FA] has agreed to extend the age to which girls can play in boys' teams to the under 13 age group from the 2010/11 season."

Yet despite the overwhelming weight of evidence and the support of the FA Council and the FA Executive, the shareholders once more refused to sanction the proposal at the FA Shareholders' AGM and the rule change was rejected again.

No official reason was given at the time, but someone who was present at the meeting told me that it was because the shareholders were concerned that clubs would have to build entirely new changing facilities to accommodate female players. If that's true then I think that shows just how out of touch the FA is with grassroots football.

It all reminded me of a scene from the 1981 film *Gregory's Girl*, which is the story of a female footballer called Dorothy who joins the school team. The side is rubbish and Dorothy ends up being the best player. A lot of the comedy revolves around people's shock reaction to a girl being good at football. Back then it would have been much more unusual to find a girl playing football, but it couldn't have happened in real life. In the movie Dorothy is supposed to be 16, so she wouldn't have been allowed to play.

In the scene, the headmaster finds out there's a girl playing in the school team and he calls Phil Menzies, the P.E teacher, into his office to explain what is going on. The headmaster doesn't give anything away at first, so Menzies tries to dodge the issue until the headmaster finally puts him out of his misery by saying, "Well, I think it's an excellent idea."

Menzies relaxes immediately and starts talking about what a great player Dorothy is.

"Just one question," says the headmaster. "What are you going to do about the showers?"

Without thinking, Menzies comes straight back with the answer.

"Oh it's okay, she'll bring her own soap."

When people find out I play for a boys' team they almost always ask questions like that. Things like "Where do you go to the toilet?" or, "Where do you get changed?" It's strange because the answers seem so obvious to me and are really boring.

"What are you going to do about the showers?"

"Like everyone else, I get showered at home."

"Where do you go to the toilet?"

"In the ladies."

"Where do you get changed?"

"At home. Like everyone else, I turn up in my kit."

I wonder what people expect me to say when they ask these questions.

"Actually, one of the rules is that we all have to use the same changing room and toilets, otherwise you're not allowed to play."

In all the years I've been playing, there's only been one occasion when players didn't turn up to the match in their kit. And even then it didn't present a problem. It was when I played for Sheffield Wednesday Boys' Elite Player Development Centre, who didn't let you take your kit home. In those games, I got changed on my own and Dad checked when it was okay for me to go into the boys' changing room for the team talk. Alternatively, I could have got changed in the car. And if all else had failed, I'm an expert at putting a shirt on under my jacket. It's not exactly a showstopper.

Unfortunately, all of this was news to the sport's governing body and finding it out had taken them four years, during which time girls elsewhere in Europe were playing mixed football – sometimes into adult life – without any problems. In Scotland, France and Portugal girls can play up to under 15; those in Germany and Italy to under 17; in Belgium to under 18; Switzerland and Holland to under 19; and in Denmark, Spain, Northern Ireland and Poland there is no upper age limit at all.

In 2011, after yet another year of research, the FA discovered what everyone playing grassroots football already knew: players get changed at home and turn up in their kit. They finally caved in. I made it by the skin of my teeth and I was determined to make the most of the opportunity.

Another more interesting question I get asked all the time is "How does boys' football compare with the girls' game?" People who've never watched girls' football assume that it must be either rubbish or inferior to the boys' game. I think it all depends on what games you're comparing.

As a whole, I hope this book will give you the answer, but if you want the headlines I would say that in both football is played to a very high standard at the top level, but at the bottom it's fairly poor. The big difference is that girls' football is a minority sport. Remember in 2005 there were 130,000 girls and women registered as players in England? Well in the Sheffield and Hallamshire Boys' Leagues alone there were around 15,000 registered players. The upshot of this is that the distance from the top to the bottom is much wider in boys' football. In girls' football, the spread of ability within a single division can be the same as it is across an entire boys' league. So it's not a question of boys v girls. Compare any league in the world containing 16 teams with one containing 76 and the same will be true regardless of whether it's boys or girls playing.

What I will say is that I found the boys' league to be much more competitive. At Rovers we usually had four or five tough games a season. At Millhouses, as I was now discovering, almost every one of our 22 matches was tough.

My first competitive game in the B League was on 4th September 2011, away to Thorncliffe Colts, a team from the north of Sheffield. Thorncliffe had finished fourth in the league the previous season, just missing out on promotion. It felt like it would be a good test.

I was again given a place in the starting 11 at left-back. By now I knew what to expect in terms of the speed of the game. Basically, you just had less time to do everything – including thinking. Thinking about putting in a tackle? Too late! Thinking about which team-mate to pass to? Too late! When you haven't got time on the ball in defence, the temptation is just to get rid of it: kick it up the pitch and hope for the best or boot it out of play. You need to work out what you're going to do with the ball before you get it.

Not long into the game it became clear to me that we were the better team and this gave me the confidence to play it short to one of the midfielders. I went off after an hour. We were winning 1-0 at the time and I was quite happy with how I had played. However, although we were on top for the whole game, we only managed to score one goal and paid the price when Colts equalised near the end.

Unfortunately, the most memorable thing about my first game had nothing to do with football. As well as the pace, the other big difference was the amount of what Dad calls 'sledging'. During matches boys are much more likely to talk to each other than girls, and not just members of their own team either. I soon discovered that mind games are a big part of boys' football.

The sledging usually starts during the pre-match handshake, which is supposedly a goodwill gesture initiated by the FA to promote sportsmanship – but that's really all it is: a gesture. My brother says he once played in an under 8 match when the biggest player from the other team whispered "F*** you!" every time he shook hands with someone.

For me it's usually something like, "Ooh! Hello Darling!" or, "Which one's your boyfriend?" or maybe a lame joke like, "Hey, I didn't know we were playing netball!" Sometimes I can't tell what they've said, but I hear them laughing about me after I've gone past. And I get wolf-whistled quite a lot. If they say something directly to me, I just roll my eyes, but if they say something to one of their mates, I just pretend I haven't heard. I don't let it bother me. I think sexist comments are inevitable, sadly.

Sometimes, when we line up for the kick-off and I'm on the side of the pitch near the spectators, I can hear the opposition parents also making jokes about me. Usually nothing too mean, but I guess they just think it's funny that a girl is playing.

Perhaps they'll say, "Make sure you get her number as you go past her" or, "Don't get distracted by the full-back."

I pretend to ignore this, but I find it really helps to get the adrenaline pumping. I'd almost go as far as to say that I like it when it happens because it gets me really fired up, especially if it's freezing cold or I'm not really in the mood for the match for some reason.

I usually go up for corners to mark the goalkeeper and I try to distract them. There was one team we played and, as I ran into the area, they all started singing, "Bird in the box! Bird in the box!" I think they were trying to put me off, but we still scored. To be honest, you do get used to it and you just have to learn how to cope. Another time I went up for a free kick and one lad said, "Why have I got to mark the girl?"

We were winning so I was feeling quite bold and said, "And why do I have to mark the dick?'

That got quite a few laughs – even from his own team-mates.

It's not all one-way though. If I flatten someone in a tackle then I always help them up, ask them if they're okay and apologise for hurting them. But really what I'm doing is making them feel worse, confirming that, yes, you really were just decked by a girl!

However, there is a point where sledging stops and abuse starts. I've never been threatened directly, but I've been called a 'slag' a few times and I've played in matches where I've heard people threaten to break someone's legs 'if you try to go past me again' or something similar. Some teams have a reputation for trying to intimidate the opposition and it's sad to say that, in my experience, they often end up succeeding. When you're playing those kinds of teams you might find that some of your own players go missing. It's little things like they stop making runs or stop calling for the ball. And when they do get it they give it away as quickly as possible.

In games like these you need leaders who'll show that they aren't scared, won't pull out of a tackle and don't really care what the other team is saying. I always try to be one of those players, as if to give the impression: 'Hey lads, if the girl isn't scared, then we don't need to be?'

Just two days after our first game against Thorncliffe Colts, we were away at Darfield in Barnsley for an evening kick-off. I was bit concerned about the referee who seemed to be the same age as us and was, rather disconcertingly, on first name terms with all the Darfield players. Again I started the match, but we went two goals down fairly quickly. About half an hour into the game, I went in for a header and got kicked in the face. My first instinct was to think, 'For God's sake, don't cry!' My second was to think, 'Ouch, that really, really hurts.'

Instead of a free kick to us the referee awarded a throw-in to them. Overwhelmed by the injustice of it all and the pain, I burst into tears and had to come off. While most of the time it feels like I'm just one of the lads, it does occasionally feel like I'm not just one of lads. This was the first of those times. If Chris or Bilal got kicked in the face and cried, it was because they got kicked in the face and it really hurt. But if I got kicked in the face and cried, it was because I'm a girl. If Dan or Sheriyar screwed up, or tried to do something and it failed to come off, it was because they weren't good enough; if I screwed up, it was because girls aren't good enough to play football. I didn't want Iain and Dave to think, 'We've made a mistake signing Niamh, this league's too tough for her', so I had a drink and told them I was ready to go back on.

It was an agonising wait through the rest of the half and half time, but with 25 minutes to go I did go back on. I was absolutely determined to show everybody that I was tough enough to play at this level, and most of all to show the winger who had kicked me in the face (and on purpose, I had decided). Within five minutes I got my chance. A 50/50 ball. I threw everything into the tackle. Sometimes, you know what's going to happen before it happens and this just felt right. I took the ball cleanly, the player went flying, and I kicked it up the pitch to Bilal who did his thing of running at 90mph past two defenders and scoring.

We ended up losing, but Iain said it was the best game I'd played.

"Perhaps we should get someone to kick you in the face before every match Niamh," he said.

It hadn't been a perfect start, but I now felt ready to take on whatever boys' football threw at me.

Chapter 8

Choices

"You can spot the girls who've been in mixed teams – their attitude is different. They seem to want it more because they've had to prove themselves. The desire seems stronger."

Faye White, former English footballer and captain of the England women's team. Finished her career with 90 caps

The first part of Iain's prediction was turning out to be true – Millhouses were slow starters. The concern was growing that we might also be slow middlers and slow finishers as well. We finally won in our third game – against the run of play – but we drew the next and then only just beat a team, in extra time, three divisions below us in the cup.

We were a goal down and I scored the equaliser from a corner. It was a tap-in from five yards after a goalmouth scramble, but they all count. This was my first goal ever in 11-a-side and given the fact it was also an equaliser in the cup, you might imagine it was something to celebrate. Unfortunately, none of us really knew what to do.

Some kids have their celebrations worked out. Bilal, who scored a lot, used to run up the pitch as fast as he could. No one could catch him so it looked pretty cool. I'd never scored before so I was really excited and desperate to celebrate. I turned round and Dan was the first player I saw. We both seemed to realise at the same time that hugs might be a bit awkward, so instead I made do with a high five and few 'nice-ones' from the rest of the team. It was all bit subdued and I was afraid it might have looked a bit insulting to the opposition, like we expected to win or something.

Iain told us to build on this platform, but the following Wednesday at training the platform sort of collapsed. First of all Bilal injured his knee and would be out for a month, and secondly Callum, who was one of two other full-backs in the squad, picked a fight with Dan. This was a surprise for two reasons. Firstly, Callum was quite quiet. I could tell he wasn't very happy about competing for a place with a girl, or anyone at all. He wasn't hostile or unfriendly, just not friendly, but he didn't strike me as the fighting type. Callum fancied himself as a striker and saw Bilal's injury as an opportunity to stake a claim for the now vacant role of match-winner, so in the practice game he went up front. He looked out of position to me and Dan kept taking the ball off him. I could see Callum was getting more and more frustrated and when it happened a third time he squared up to Dan.

This was the second surprise because Dan really *was* the fighting type: a County boxer and the biggest and strongest player in the squad. So if Callum really wanted a fight he'd picked on the right person in that sense. He threw the first punch and I wondered if I'd underestimated him. But after a couple of return punches, it was obvious that I hadn't and that Dan was going to batter him. Iain and Dave broke up the fight quickly enough, but Callum stormed off and that was the last we saw of him. Dan acted as if nothing had happened and neither the fight nor Callum was ever mentioned again.

On a practical level the squad was now down to just 12 players, but we only had two full-backs so at least I was now guaranteed a full game almost every week. Every cloud...

We lost the next match 3-0 (they took their chances, we didn't). And with only 11 fit players it was starting to look like it might be a long and difficult season. Then everything changed.

Ben joined in Callum's place. He was another full-back and one of the best headers of the ball I'd ever seen. We won our next two games 4-1 and 6-2. The new players had settled in – me included – and the small squad meant that the same team played week in, week out. Without Bilal, the long ball over the top wasn't an option so we started playing the ball shorter, through the midfield, and were a better team as a consequence. More players were scoring goals, and we also had the tightest defence in the whole league, from division A to G.

When Bilal returned we just carried on playing the same way. We won every match in October and November, by which time we were going out expecting to win every game and felt unbeatable. By the end of the month we were second in the league following seven straight wins.

I was learning quite a few things about my team-mates. Football aside, it really wasn't like playing for a girls' team at all. I was finding out first hand how boys interacted with each other and there were a few surprises. One was how competitive they were about everything, no matter how unimportant it was.

For example, with so few parents coming to watch, transport for away games was always a problem and Iain would be constantly trying to sort lifts for everyone. If Dad or Mum were coming to watch, we'd usually be picking up two or three lads on the way. There was always a scramble for the best seats. In this respect, being the only girl was a huge advantage. One lad would call 'shotgun' and grab hold of the front door handle while the others tried to push him out of the way and prise his hand open. Meanwhile, those in the back would try to spread out and secure as much space for themselves as possible. And no one ever wanted to sit in the middle – the worst place of all, reserved for the lowest members of 'the pack'.

None of that applied to me though. I'd nearly always get the front seat, and on the rare occasions I did have to squeeze into the back of Dave's Alfa Romeo, I'd never be in the middle. I would always be guaranteed loads of space, as whoever pulled the short straw and ended up next to me tried desperately hard to avoid any bodily contact.

I'd initially thought they were reluctant to speak to me because they didn't want to, but I began to realise that it was because they didn't know how to. In an odd way, I think lads at this age find girls a bit intimidating. Every week to start the warm-up, Iain would get us to play a game of 'Chain-Tig' in the centre circle, in which each person 'tigged' (or 'tagged') would have to hold hands and form a chain. I won this game every single week. I didn't even need to try and get out of the way, because absolutely no one wanted to be seen joining hands with me.

But at the same time, my team-mates seemed to like having a girl in the team. No one ever had a go at me for not being good enough or not trying hard enough, and they always shouted good things when I won the ball or made a pass. I found all this really encouraging, but don't think I'd stumbled across a team full of new men.

It's fair to say that the lads at Millhouses were very confident in their own ability: not bad lads at all, but definitely pretty cocky. Not without good reason though. The team was full of quick, skilful, flair players and they are always the cockiest: the sort who can take you on and beat you from a standing start. Once they were satisfied that I was a good player too, they started to realise that this might reflect really well on them. There was a lot of teams from Sheffield in our division, so we would often be playing against boys from the same group of schools as ourselves. Having me in the team gave our side extra bragging rights. It was as if we were saying to the opposition, 'Ha! We're so much better than you. Not only can we beat you, but we can do it with a girl in our team!'

The next day in school they'd 'remind' their mates that 'Niamh, the girl in our team' had tackled them. That kind of arrogance is harder to find in the girls' game, but in my experience it comes naturally to boys. Arrogance can either be positive or negative, but in this case it was definitely the former. But we were winning games, and when you're winning games team spirit is always pretty good. It's when you're getting beaten every week that people start pointing the finger.

While everything at Millhouses was going well for me, there was also a problem: the season was going past too quickly. It was only November, but we were already approaching the midway stage. The question of where I was going to play the following year was starting to become a concern. I didn't need anyone to tell me how much I'd improved as a player during my time at Millhouses – I could feel it. I was playing quicker, my touch had improved, I was more vocal, better in the air and more comfortable on the ball. Millhouses were now second in the league and promotion to the top division – the A League – looked a distinct possibility. That would have been a real achievement, but I wouldn't be able to take advantage of it. I really wanted to progress, but as the rules stood I'd be going back to grassroots girls' football at the end of the season. That didn't feel like progress at all.

I talked to my dad about it and he said he'd contact the FA, but said that it was, "In hope rather than expectation. It took them four years to raise the age limit to 13, so I wouldn't get excited just yet."

The first person he contacted was Gemma, the Women's Football Development Officer at the Sheffield and Hallamshire FA. Dad sent her an email explaining the situation and asked if there were any plans to extend the age limit to under 14 at the end of the season. She said that the age limit would definitely not be extended at the end of the season, but I "could always join a team in the girls' league." She did also offer to arrange a trial at Sheffield United CoE. I really didn't want a trial there, so Dad wrote back and said thanks but no thanks. And that was that.

Or so we thought.

The next day at work, Dad got a phone call from Rachel Pavlou at the FA. She was really sympathetic but confirmed that it was, "Highly unlikely that the mixed football age limit will be extended again.

"I am trying to change minds here, but it's very difficult and I think it might be too late for Niamh. It's seen as a health and safety issue more than anything else."

She also said that the FA's research was ongoing and asked if I'd like to be included in it. And she said she did have a possible alternative for me, playing-wise.

"We've just completely revised the whole Centre of Excellence system. How far is Derby County from you? I'd be very happy to organise a trial for Niamh there if you'd like me to. That could be a good alternative for her next season."

Later that day Dad received a call from Derby County. It was from the Centre Director, Peter Johnson, who invited me to take part in a training session.

"I think it would be really good if Niamh came down. It's not a trial as such, I know she's no plans to leave her club until the end of the season, but it would be a chance for her to check us out and see what she thinks. It's also a chance for us to get to know her ahead of the trials next June."

When I got in from school it seemed like an awful lot had happened. Rachel sent us through some information about CoEs, which were part of 'The FA Player Pathway' from grassroots to the England team.

At the start of 'The Player Pathway' were the various grassroots leagues and Player Development Centres (PDCs, which sounded a lot like the old development squad at Sheffield United). These fed into 29 CoEs across the country, catering for a small number of 'elite players'.

Unlike in grassroots, these age groups were based on birth

year rather than school year. So, because my birthday is the 13th December, this meant that even though I was only 12, I would be playing in the under 15 age group. A lot of the players would be two school years older than me. If I'd been born just a few weeks later I'd have been in the under 13s.

There were so many rules, but the five most important appeared to be:

1. If you joined a CoE you couldn't play for anyone else and you could only leave with the FA's permission
2. Up to under 17 there were no leagues: all matches were friendlies and all squad players must play an equal number of minutes over the course of the season
3. There was four hours' training a week, split into two sessions
4. Matches were played against other CoEs on Saturdays
5. No CoE team was allowed to play a grassroots team

The big selling point appeared to be that only players from CoEs could play for England. The brochure said that scouts would regularly attend matches and the best players would be invited to training camps. The England squad selection would be based on the performances at those camps.

There was a lot to take in and I wasn't sure it was for me. If I could have chosen, I'd have definitely stayed at Millhouses, but I could see that this would probably be my best option for the next season. There was also the fact that the FA seemed to be saying that attending a CoE was the only route to becoming a professional women's footballer. I wasn't sure why that was, but assumed it was due to the standard of football being played. With that in mind, I thought I'd have to go and at least check it out.

I went the following evening. Derby's training ground was 35 miles away and it took about 50 minutes to get there. Everybody was really friendly. Natasha, the centre manager, took me over me to the under 15 coaches, Dan and Charlotte.

"So you're the girl who's been playing with boys are you?" said Dan. "Good for you."

They introduced me to the squad. After trialing with all the boys' teams this wasn't very scary, especially as no one was surprised to see a girl turn up, sniggering or making lame jokes. I also realised that I actually knew a couple of the players already. Beth and Bronwyn were two years older than me, but had also been in Sheffield United's development squad, so I joined in with them at first.

The session was good. It was quite technical – which I liked. It was like the training at Sheffield United but with a clearer purpose. Dan and Charlotte were obviously preparing a team for a game rather than just coaching a bunch of players. The standard was pretty good and players generally had a better understanding of their roles than in grassroots. Even at Millhouses there was a tendency for players to hold on to the ball for too long. That's the benefit of coaching, I guess, and even though this was my first session, I could see that Dan and Charlotte were trying to get the team to defend as a unit: with full-backs tucking in to the centre-backs rather than pushing out wide to mark the wingers.

The biggest difference between girls' grassroots and CoE football, though, was in attitude. There was no mucking about at all – which again I really liked. No talking when the coach was explaining something, there was no texting (mobile phones were banned) and everyone was trying their best to complete the drills. Girls were here to learn how to play football.

At the end of training Charlotte asked me to bring my dad over so she could have a quick chat.

"She did very well," said Charlotte. "Both Dan and myself think Niamh's exactly the kind of player we're looking for, and if you're happy, we'd like to sign her tonight and put her into the squad to face Stoke on Saturday."

I couldn't believe what I'd just heard. I thought we were just checking each other out. I'd spent a year in the development squad at Sheffield United's CoE and never got near the squad, but here I was being offered a place after my first training session. I was very flattered and quite excited. Of course I wanted to join the squad to face Stoke on Saturday! Of course I wanted to sign… but hang on, what about Millhouses? Would I have to give them up?

Dad seemed to be thinking along the same lines.

"Wow!" he said. "That's a bit of a shock, we didn't know this was a trial, or that you even had a space in the squad. Thanks very much, but I think it's just a lot for Niamh to take in, that's all. It's a big decision to make. There's the travelling to consider too."

"Sure, I understand," replied Charlotte. "We've got 15 players signed, but we can go to 18. We're looking for one more and we're short of defenders, so Niamh is the perfect fit really."

Dad looked at me.

"The thing is, Niamh's signed for a boys' team this season. She's happy there and the plan was to stay with them until the end of the season."

I nodded vigorously.

"They play on Sundays, so I don't suppose there's any way she could play for them as well is there?"

I was praying for Charlotte to say yes.

"No she can't, I'm afraid. Once she signs for us, that's it. She can't play at grassroots any more. Even if it is for a boys' team."

"Can she think about it overnight and get back to you tomorrow?" said Dad.

"Sure, I appreciate it's a big decision and we've got a game against Man United next week. So if Saturday is too soon, you can think about making your debut in that game instead."

Playing against Manchester United did sound amazing.

"The thing to remember," said Charlotte, "is what a big opportunity this is. If you want to be a footballer, this is the place to be. This is where all the elite players are: the top 400 girls in your age group. We have England scouts coming all the time – there was one here last weekend. You could be literally only weeks away from a call-up. If you're not playing at a Centre of Excellence you can't play for England."

That did sound encouraging. I had never considered that I'd be remotely good enough to play for England, but Charlotte was making it sound possible – achievable even. Yet I was sure I didn't want to give up playing for Millhouses.

On the way home we talked about what to do. We went backwards and forwards weighing everything up, but in the morning I made a decision. I would be staying with Millhouses. Derby County sounded fantastic, but if I waited until the end of the season I'd still be an under 15 (and no longer be the youngest in the group either). What's more, I would be playing with girls for the rest of my life, so this season was the last opportunity to play for a boys' team. I wanted to stay and win promotion, if possible – to achieve something with the team. I also didn't want to leave Iain in the lurch after he'd taken a chance on me. If I went, they'd be left with only 12 players.

Dad rang Charlotte to let her know. He said I was very grateful, but I'd made a commitment to Millhouses and didn't want to let them down. Also the original plan had been to try out for Derby at the end of the season, so we'd like to stick to that. Charlotte said she was disappointed, but understood where I was coming from.

That evening, Charlotte called again. The coaches had held a discussion and, although they understood the situation with Millhouses, they said they still really wanted me to join Derby.

"So we've come up with a compromise," said Charlotte. "As a Centre of Excellence we're allowed to have players on a six-week trial. So rather than sign you today, we could delay that for six weeks, during which time you can carry on playing for your club, and they'll have a decent amount of time to find a replacement."

We talked it over. This would still mean I'd miss 11 league games – the whole of the second half of the season. But it was *only* 11 games. Everyone we asked was telling me there'd be no more mixed football at under 14 level. If I said 'no', I'd be giving up the chance of going to a CoE – possibly forever – for just 11 matches. Given that the FA had pretty much said there would be no chance of playing with the boys next season and that getting this quality of coaching was the only way for me to become good enough to be a professional footballer, I felt like there was only one decision to take. I didn't want to leave. It would kill me to leave Millhouses, but I was going to have to.

Iain was really sad when I told him, but said he understood that it was good opportunity for me. And with just 12 fit players he was very relieved that he'd have six weeks to find a replacement. I tried not to think about leaving – it just made me sad too. Instead, I tried to follow the advice of a million post-match interviews and 'take each game as it comes'.

Chapter 9
A Game of Three Halves

"Let the women play in more feminine clothes like they do in volleyball. They could, for example, have tighter shorts. Female players are pretty, if you excuse me for saying so, and they already have some different rules to men – such as playing with a lighter ball. That decision was taken to create a more female aesthetic, so why not do it in fashion?"

Sepp Blatter, President of FIFA

There are some big differences between grassroots and academy or Centre of Excellence football. Training at Millhouses wasn't bad at all. We didn't just have a kickabout; we did proper drills and were coached. But in just one hour a week we didn't really have the chance to learn much. At Derby the coaches were not necessarily better qualified (both Dave at Millhouses and Charlotte at Derby were at Level 2), but they had much more time to spend working with the players. Sessions were well organised and the coaches could go into great detail about how they wanted you to play and had the time to take you through elaborate or more challenging drills.

All the CoEs use the official FA coaching system, which in theory teaches you how to play the kind of football you see in the Premier League. The emphasis is usually on possession, playing the ball out from the back and defending and attacking as a unit. In grassroots, you'll hear spectators shouting advice like, "Get stuck in!", "Get rid of it!", "Let him know you're there" or, "If in doubt, kick it out." I'd often hear someone shout at me to mark the winger tight, even if he was standing out wide doing nothing and I was tucked in next to the centre-back, in the right place to deal with whatever might happen. At Derby, the advice was always, "Don't dive in!" "Stay on your feet!" "Keep hold of the ball!" "Don't give it away!"

Gaining a technical understanding of the game was good, but the actual football at Derby was not a step-up at all. The spread of ability within the squad was the biggest surprise. I joined with the view that it was going to be a much higher level than I'd ever played before, but as the weeks went by it became clear that there was actually a bigger spread of ability in the squad than anywhere else I'd played. There were some very good players, with one or two on the verge of the England squad, but there were quite a few not-so-good players too. In my opinion, some would have struggled to get into Middlewood Rovers' squad, while there were three Rovers players who could have made a real difference to the Derby side.

We trained twice a week. Monday's session was all about fitness. Although I never found the fitness sessions themselves to be much of a problem (in these drills I was always in the top two or three), Charlotte and Dan complained that the squad wasn't fit enough. This was true in a few cases, but I know they didn't feel my fitness was a problem. Spending almost two hours commuting just to run round a football pitch because some of our players couldn't last a full game... well it was hard not to become a bit demotivated.

Thursday evenings were much more enjoyable, simply because we did a lot more work with the ball in preparation for the game at the weekend. Derby's style was more direct than Millhouses'. The focus was on getting the ball forwards quickly and out wide to the wingers. The theory was that they would get behind the full-backs and cross it in to the box.

Every single pass was to be played forwards. This meant we often gave the ball away (too much in my opinion), so the coaches worked on holding our shape so we'd be in a position to win it back.

The matches themselves were different to anything I'd played before. They were all friendlies and the scores weren't recorded. Occasionally we'd finish a game and no one would know what the final score was. The coaches rarely mentioned the result. Matches were played over three periods of 25 minutes (we still called them halves) and every player in the squad had to be given an equal amount of pitch time over the course of the season.

The idea was that it was all in aid of player development and was similar to the way that boys' academies are run. I can't speak for them but, for me at least, this set-up provided some surprising consequences. For example, we had two goalkeepers, Cassie and Ellen, who each played half a match. Cassie was way better than Ellen in every respect. So whenever we changed goalkeeper we had to completely change the way we played as a defence. For half the match we'd have a keeper who came for crosses, was very vocal, commanded her area and provided an option to pass back too. For the other, we'd have one who was nervous, stayed on her line, was poor in the air and uncomfortable on the ball. Everyone seemed to be waiting for her to make a mistake and, unfortunately, they usually didn't have to wait long.

My first game for Derby was away to Man United. I was given a place in the starting line-up at left-back. At kick-off, we could see how Man United were set up. And one thing I noticed immediately was just how big the left-winger was. She was about 5ft 9in, powerfully built and looked fully grown. She was like a female Wayne Rooney. Megan, who was playing at centre-back, warned me to watch her, "She's in the England under 15s. She's really fast and fouls all the time."

It struck me that the people at the FA who thought mixed football at under 14 was a health and safety issue might like to come and watch me – a 12-year-old – get flattened in this under 15 girls' match.

The winger turned out to be the one outstanding player on the pitch. The first 50/50 we had I hesitated and she skinned me. I hate to say it now, but I was intimidated. It's funny, playing with lads week in week out I hadn't expected to feel like that. But the truth is that when someone much bigger, stronger and faster than you is running at you, the fact that they're a girl doesn't make it any less painful when they smash into you.

I was determined not to let that happen again, so I made sure I got right behind her. About 10 minutes later she received the ball 20 yards out, near the corner of our penalty area. I was marking her really tightly and thought, 'You're not going anywhere this time.' But she brought the ball down with her first touch, span round and, with her second touch, fired it into the top corner of our goal. 1-0 to Man United.

I didn't really have an answer to her, but then no one on our team did. She scored three and set another up before half time. We managed to pull a goal back to go in 4-1 down at the first break. I'd played so badly I felt like crying. I tried to keep it in. At least I wasn't the only one. I was expecting us to get a rollocking from the coach about our performance to fire us up for the second half, but everybody was really calm. Too calm.

"Why are you upset Niamh, you've done a good job of coping with a really strong opponent," said Dan.

"Thanks, but I don't feel like I'm having a good game," I said.

"No, you're playing well – you all are. Remember she's almost two years older than you," said Charlotte.

They might have meant it, but we were on the same pitch so that wasn't an excuse. I'd have been really annoyed if Iain had said, "Don't worry Niamh, that winger who's skinning you every time is a boy after all". They may have just been nice because it was my first game, but I felt like they were just making up excuses.

I've played in several games since where there has been one outstanding player in the opposition running riot. There is always some advice from the manager at half time about how to contain them. Maybe motivational, along the lines of, 'They've only got one good lad and none of you will put a challenge in! Here's what we're going to do about it...'. But today there was nothing. There was no, 'You need to do this and you shouldn't be doing that'. There was no advice or change of plan at all for the second half. Some people came off because of the equal minutes thing, but the half-time team talk was just, "These are a strong team, keep doing what you're doing and don't worry about the result."

They just seemed to accept that none of us would be good enough to match up to her.

"Is there anything more I should be doing to stop her?" I asked, hoping for some advice on positioning or confirmation of when to put a challenge in.

"Not really," said Dan, "just keep going and don't worry about it."

I played much better in the second period, but that was due to the fact that 'Rooney' had been taken off. Without her Man United seemed to have a similar spread of ability to Derby and we managed to get back in the game at 4-3. They took me off at the second break, but the equal minutes thing made it unclear whether it had anything to do with my performance.

'Rooney' came back on for the final third and it was obvious that no one on our team could cope with her. With our own best striker, Rhian, also on the pitch, there was an exchange of goals and the final score finished 8-5 to United.

I was feeling a bit shellshocked. I'd never played for a team that had conceded more than three goals in a match before. I hadn't played well, but it seemed clear to me that our defence had been all over the place.

On the way home I spoke to Dad. He said that, despite what Dan and Charlotte had said, he didn't think I'd played well, but said he thought no one on our side had apart from Rhian. He said he noticed that I had bottled the first challenge, but no one else had coped with that winger.

"You should want to play against good players like that though. It's the only way you'll improve" he said.

For once I thought he was right. I've always pushed myself to be the best player I can and I felt I'd let myself down. More than anything else now, I wanted to play Man United again next week and make sure that I got the upper hand next time.

When you've had a bad game the next one can't come quick enough, so I was really glad to be playing again for Millhouses the following day. We were up against Sheffield Sixes again, but this time in the regional quarter-finals of the Tesco Cup, which is a national competition for under 13 teams.

It felt good to be back in a team playing well. I put the previous day's match behind me and tried as hard as I could from the off. It was a tight game, which only seemed to make what was always going to be a physical match much tougher, but we got our noses in front just after half time and finished up 2-0 winners. This time I didn't need anyone else to tell me I'd played well – I knew I had.

And so began a cycle of training twice a week, losing with Derby on Saturday and winning with Millhouses on Sunday. While Charlotte and Dan were good at coaching, I was less convinced about the way they managed the team. Coaching and managing are two very different things. A coach teaches you how to play football; a manager sets the side up and tells you what to do to win matches. Derby's matches were usually high-scoring games and the main reason for this was that everyone had to have an equal amount of pitch time.

This meant that you couldn't just play your strongest side. How well we did depended entirely on who's turn it was to be on the pitch. For example, in our second match against Everton I played in the first half, which we won 3-2. For the second, I sat on the bench along with Cassie, the good goalkeeper, and Megan, our best centre-back. We lost that one 6-0.

To me all these rules seemed to be making it very difficult to get the defence organised. It probably works fine in boys' academies, where all the players are of an appropriate standard. But in girls' CoEs, with their two-year age groups, lack of scouting and other factors, there is a much bigger spread of ability.

There was one girl called Piper, who was noticeably struggling. Piper was very nice, but she wasn't the quickest, lacked a confident first touch, was very quiet on the pitch, had no positional sense and couldn't pass the ball. Piper was a centre-back. Playing alongside her at full-back, you could never be sure that she was in the right position and quickly learned that it was dangerous to pass to her. Whenever she was on the pitch at the same time as the weaker goalkeeper, it rained goals.

In one game away at Liverpool, I was on the bench for the first half. I noticed Megan and Cassie were also subs. 'At least I'll be playing with them in the second half,' I thought.

When it got to half time we were losing 8-0.

"Forget about the score. Treat it as 0-0 when you go on," said Dan.

I was sure that that was the right attitude, but you could see that quite a few of the players didn't want to go back out for the second half at all. For those of us coming on it was a bit difficult to motivate ourselves knowing that winning the match was impossible. In the end we got beaten 10-3, but although we had – as our coaches were quick to point out – 'won the second half', it didn't feel like much of an achievement and it was very difficult to stay focused.

All in all I was beginning to think, 'And I've given up playing boys' football for this!'

Millhouses games were always better, and I was really enjoying being in the same league as the boys from my school. The captain of the school team, Chris, was in my form and he played for Thorncliffe Juniors (not to be confused with Thorncliffe Colts) who were in the same division as us. Chris was a very good player. His team had been relegated from the A League and he was confident about going straight back up.

I got on well with Chris, but his team won their first seven games so Millhouses' slow start gave him the opportunity to take the mickey. And he made the most of it. He'd bring up our impending fixture at every opportunity.

"Oh, I can't wait until we play you," he'd say. "You do realise we're going to absolutely hammer you, don't you?"

"Sure you will," I'd say.

"You might have a load of 20 year olds playing for you Niamh, but we'll still batter you."

Whenever we were dropping points he'd be straight in on Monday morning.

"Couldn't believe your result yesterday. You must be worse than I thought if you can't beat them."

I really enjoyed this. Chris may have imagined that he was getting to me, but I just thought it was brilliant that the captain of the school team was taking the trouble to look up my team's results on the internet. He'd never been interested in any football I'd played before. The taunting intensified as the game approached. By the time we played each other his team were top of the league after seven straight wins and 10 points ahead of us in second place. It all made me really up for it.

We won the match easily, 3-0, and I had my own put-downs worked out in advance. When I got into class, Chris was sitting with his three best mates, who'd all been laughing along with him for weeks. They already knew the result and started smiling as I walked up behind him.

"Alright, Chris? Did you enjoy the weekend? I know I did."

They all burst out laughing.

"Yeah, but we should have definitely had a penalty," said Chris.

Late in the game, with the score at 3-0, Thorncliffe had had a penalty appeal turned down. I knew he'd mention that.

"I can see why you wanted a penalty Chris, because you needed all the help you could get against our team, didn't you?"

Even Chris started laughing now. He knew there was no coming back from that. At this point I was really grateful for all his teasing over the previous weeks: it had made victory feel even better.

That result really made a big difference to how I was perceived by the lads in my year. Chris was really respected for his ability, but I'd beaten him and his team, so people started respecting me as a player too. I wasn't just making up the numbers in a struggling lower league side: I was a starter in one of the best teams in the city. That really did fill me with confidence.

For the time being, Sundays remained the highlight of my week. Millhouses won every match in November and December, but for me the games were running out. Six soon became two, and before I knew it I was playing my final match, just before the Christmas break.

I would like to say it was an emotional moment when

I left, but remember this was an under 13 boys' team. So although I did get a card and a present (a box of chocolates and a Millhouses shirt with my name on the back) following our 7-0 dismantling of Wickersley, there was not much more than a few goodbye grunts from my team-mates. However, to say I was sorry to be leaving would be an understatement: I was devastated.

Derby, meanwhile, were yet to win a game since I had joined, but nobody seemed at all bothered. The coaches kept hammering home that the result didn't matter. They would occasionally have a go at people if they thought they really weren't pulling their weight or putting the effort in, but there was never a radical change of tactics or attempt to try something different either.

No one would ever admit to wanting to win the game. Every week we just went out onto the pitch and got battered. Occasionally, you'd hear someone say, "Come on! They're not that much better than us," but there was no, "Get your head in the game! Let's have a winner!"

People were never critical either. If somebody made a mistake – which happened quite a lot – everyone would try to gee them up by saying, "Don't worry about it. It doesn't matter."

I suppose that's quite nice to hear, but sometimes I think you do need a kick in the pants. It was hard not to contrast this reaction with what happened if someone at Millhouses missed a sitter or gave a goal away. Usually it was something like, "For f***'s sake, we've got to be better than that!" or "Come on lads, do we want this?" It really did keep you on your toes and give you a lift.

By the same token, if you did something good the boys were more likely to acknowledge it: "Keep playing that ball"' or "You've done him!" or "Great challenge!" There was an edge at Millhouses that was missing at Derby. It wasn't that the lads weren't nice, it was just that winning seemed to be much more important to them. Without exception, everyone was very nice at Derby, but I'd have swapped it for less-nice-and-caring-more-about-winning.

As the weeks went by, even the training stopped being enjoyable. I was so conscious of the opportunity I'd been given that I didn't say anything about this at all, but the hour-long commute to run round a pitch or prepare for another massacre quickly lost its appeal. The novelty of 'elite football' was fast wearing off.

Rather than miss playing over the Christmas break, for the first time in my life I really enjoyed not having to go to training or play matches. Even when we won our first game back in January, a 1-0 victory against Stoke, I didn't think, 'Yay, we've won a game!' but rather, 'How bad must you lot be if you lost to us?'

At the next training session, Dan singled me out for faint praise.

"Niamh won every header on Saturday," he said. "She's the youngest in the team, so if she can head the ball why can't the rest of you? How can you call yourselves elite footballers if you won't head the ball?"

This really didn't do much for my ego – "If Niamh can…" – but then what about the players who wouldn't head the ball? I couldn't agree more, but I found it hard to imagine Iain having to make the same speech.

The following weekend we played Man United at their place again. I'd been waiting for this fixture since that first match: a chance for me to prove to myself that I was good enough. At training on Thursday I asked Dan if he'd consider playing me at left-back so I could go up against 'Rooney'.

"That's the kind of attitude I like," he said. "Somebody who likes a challenge. I'll definitely bear that in mind."

On Saturday morning I got up at 6:45am. We left home at 7:30am for the 11am kick-off in Salford. It was one of those cold, grey, drizzly days that Manchester is famous for, but I was definitely up for it. After the warm-up Dan named the team. I wasn't going to start.

"I want to see where they're going to play her first and then we can bring you on against her," explained Dan.

It seemed like a plan. As it turned out, for the first third, 'Rooney' wasn't on the pitch either. It gave me a chance to watch the game. Piper had been moved to midfield with the instruction to play in front of the centre-backs and break-up play.

"Try to impose yourself on the game," Charlotte had told her.

Man United seemed to have improved since we last played them. Certainly they played a very different game to us. It was all about possession, passing it across the back four and the midfield. We weren't getting much of the ball and when we did, we were just giving it straight back. Our midfield was overrun. Piper was visibly struggling with the pace of the game. Our other central midfielder, Toni, was scampering about trying her best, but United always seemed to have an outlet and she was chasing shadows.

"I wish I had 11 players like Toni," said Charlotte to Dan as our midfield was bypassed yet again.

By the end of the first third, United were winning 3-0, but it could have been worse. For their second goal I counted 22 passes.

Dan made some changes at the first break, but I stayed on the bench. 'Rooney' came on the pitch and, as before, ran riot. At the second break it was 7-0 to United, but I was still on the bench. I was bored and frustrated. I was used to fighting for my place in the team, but here there was no point. Spending the whole match warming up was bad enough, but watching the team get annihilated when I'd been so up for the game was a real let down.

With 10 minutes to go Dan brought me on at right-back.

'Rooney' was on the opposite wing, so there was going to be no personal rematch. But with the score now 8-0, it was a bit difficult to find the motivation. There were no specific instructions, just, "You've played a lot recently Niamh, so have a bit of a run out and enjoy yourself."

I felt like asking him, "What is the point?" You didn't have to earn a place in this team, you just took a turn. I tried to stay positive, as at least it meant I'd get a full game the following week.

We got back to Sheffield at 2:30pm and just had time to grab a sandwich before rushing off to watch Sheffield United. I felt like I had wasted seven hours of the weekend for 10 minutes of rubbish football!

"At least you got to play," joked Dad. "I had the pleasure of driving for four hours on my day off to watch other people's kids play football."

I told him what Charlotte had said about having 11 players like Toni.

"That figures," he said. "The way she sets the team up, you can see she loves her runners. I suppose Toni does always try hard."

With no football on Sunday mornings anymore, I decided against a lie-in and went to watch my brother play instead. Rather than being a substitute for having a match myself, watching his team just made me feel more frustrated. During the game Dad got a phone call.

"It's from Iain. That's nice he must be ringing to let us know how Millhouses got on," he said.

"Hi Steve, I'm really sorry to call and I know it's a long shot, but would Niamh be willing to play for us this afternoon? We've only got 10 players. I know it's a lot to ask – I don't want to get anyone into trouble – but she's still registered and we're desperate. I'll completely understand if it's a no. Kick-off's in 45 minutes."

Dad turned to me.

"Look, this is your decision, but Iain's asking if…"

"I'll play!"

"… I mean I don't think Derby will find out…"

"I'll play!"

"… but they wouldn't be very happy about it if…"

"I don't care! I'll play! I'll play! Let's go."

I was so happy to be going back. A lift home was arranged for Evan as we dashed across town to Millhouses' pitch. On the way I rang Mum, who met us in the car park with my kit. I got changed in the car and made it onto the pitch with just five minutes to spare.

"I can't thank you enough," said Iain. "We're absolutely desperate. Guido has been picked to play basketball for England, so we were already without a keeper. Ben injured his hip at training on Wednesday and is out for the season and Luke called in sick this morning. Niamh, can you play left-back please?"

Today's game was against Junior Blades: Sheffield United's community team. We might have only had 11 players, and been without our goalkeeper, but otherwise it was still a strong line-up.

I'd been in too much of a panic to get ready in time to take any notice of the opposition, but now as we lined up for the handshake I could see Junior Blades were all laughing about something. I wondered briefly what they were finding so funny, then I realised: it was me!

Teams usually arrive about half an hour to 45 minutes before kick-off. During the warm-up, Blades were bound to have realised that Millhouses only had 10 players. Coming to play a tough away match and finding your opponents only have 10 men would have given them a real morale boost. And then finding out that the 11th 'man' turning up five minutes before kick-off was actually a girl… well, I could kind of see their point.

But I couldn't have cared less. I was back were I wanted to

be: playing with the boys again. And it was where I wanted to stay.

Chapter 10
The Secret Footballer

"I have always played with boys since the beginning, and sometimes with boys who were a little older than me – and I noticed that I was always standing out. So when I got to that point, I noticed I was pretty good."

Marta, Brazilian footballer and the world's top paid female player in 2014

We won the game against Junior Blades 3-2, but it was more comfortable than it sounds. With a regular goalkeeper we'd have won 3-0. It had felt great to be playing with Millhouses again, not just because we won the game but because we were such a good team. We weren't waiting for each other to make mistakes. Although I understood the reason for only playing friendlies at Derby, I missed playing in matches like this where the result mattered. Winning isn't the be all and end all, but it is important. Football is a game after all.

Iain was really pleased with the performance.

"That was a real team effort," he said.

"Is Niamh back?" asked Dan. "I thought you'd left to go to an academy or something."

"It's probably just a one off because we were short," said Iain. "And thanks so much for helping us out, Niamh. They're obviously coaching you well at Derby, you had a super game."

"I'll definitely play again next week... if you're still short," I said.

It was bad enough leaving once, I didn't want to go again. I mean, I'd just played a game, I was a registered player. Who was really going to be bothered? Dad had the answer.

"You're not breaking any rules in this league, but I think the people who would be upset about this are Derby," he said.

"I don't care if they get angry. What's the worst they could do?" I replied.

"Kick you out. If they found out they could kick you out. They might well do that."

"Do you think they will find out?"

He paused for a moment.

"If I'm honest, I don't see how they could. Sheffield United Centre of Excellence don't know who's playing in the local girls' league, so I don't think Derby are going to be running spot checks on a boys' league 40 miles away. Have Dan or Charlotte mentioned you playing for Millhouses?"

"Not since the first training session. I don't think it's crossed their mind that anyone would want to carry on playing grassroots football if they'd got a place at Derby. That might be true if you've come from girls' football, but..."

"You're not playing girls' football."

"Exactly."

"So you do want to carry on playing for Millhouses?"

"Yeah I do. And it's only a few more matches. So can I?"

"I suppose the answer is, 'No you can't, but yes you can'. As long as you know what you're getting into. In the unlikely event that Derby find out, there will be at best a very embarrassing telling off and at worst you'll get kicked out."

"That's fine with me."

"It is now, but if Derby do find out then what will you do at the end of the season when there's nowhere else to play?"

"I'm fine with that too. I'll just go back to playing for Rovers. That's not so bad. I preferred it there to Derby anyway."

"Okay then, but we're not going to lie to anyone. We can keep it quiet but if anyone asks at Derby we 'fess up' right away, okay? I'll take the blame as the irresponsible adult."

Sometimes, just occasionally, my dad is okay.

"I don't want to get anyone into trouble, but I can't say I'm not relieved to have you back," said Iain when we told him about my decision. "If you'd asked me a month ago I'd have said we were nailed on to win the league, but we've just discovered that Bilal and Sheriyar are off to Pakistan for a wedding and will be missing for six weeks.

"Ben's out for the season; Guido's got basketball now every third week so, with you, we're down to just 11 players. Munib's got a mate coming to training on Wednesday. I'm not confident he'll be a worldie, but as long as he's got two legs we'll be signing him."

And that was how I returned to the cycle of training twice a week, then losing with Derby on Saturday and winning with Millhouses on Sunday.

The threadbare Millhouses squad continued to grind out wins. Despite the loss of Bilal and Sheriyar we continued our run of straight victories in league games until April. The only match we lost was in the quarter-finals of the County Cup where, minus a goalkeeper and with only 10 players, we were beaten 1-0 by a team from the A League who converted a dubious penalty late in the game.

I didn't know whether it was the contrast between the two clubs, but I was enjoying my time at Derby less and less. Apart from the reverse fixture against Stoke, which we won 2-0, the losses kept mounting up: Liverpool, Lincoln, Everton, Blackburn – they all hammered us. The only other game we won was a 3-0 victory against Sheffield United. It was great to celebrate our biggest win of the season, but the respite was brief. The following week it was back to normal as Everton put a sackful past us. I could see why nobody kept count of the score.

Training was also becoming a real drag, especially on Mondays with the emphasis on fitness and what seemed, for me at least, a pointless hour of running round the pitch. Charlotte and Dan were concerned that we were conceding so many goals late in the game and worried that we weren't fit. They were right, a lot of us weren't fit, but I didn't think this was the way to solve the problem. I always made sure I was in the top three in every exercise, just to say, 'Look – it's not my fault', but it wasn't helping performances on Saturdays.

The dread would build up on the way home from school. I'd pray for snow in the hope that training would be cancelled or I'd think, 'If I fell over now, I could get slightly injured and then I wouldn't have to go to.' I felt bad for thinking like this and I knew it was wrong. I knew that lots of people would love an opportunity to play at Derby, that it was a privilege to be part of 'the elite', but that didn't make me enjoy it. One week it started snowing when we were on the way there and Dan called to say that training had been cancelled. We were already at Chesterfield, so to compensate for the 'disappointment' of missing training, Dad took me to see *The Hunger Games* at the cinema. I was much happier sitting in the cinema with a diet coke and popcorn rather than running round a freezing cold pitch.

Two really good things did happen at Derby, though. The first was that they sent me on a coaching course and I got my first FA coach's badge, and the second was that at the end of the season we got to play at Derby's ground, Pride Park.

The match was played at the very end of the season, straight after my one-on-one assessment. It was very much like a school parents' evening, where you are given a re-port and then, a week later, you and your parent(s) have a 10-minute progress meeting with the coaches. My report was pretty good. It said I was 'At the Required Standard' for touch, technique and passing, and 'Above the Required Standard' for positioning, heading and ball-winning. I got top marks for attitude and effort, which pleased Mum much more than anything to do with my actual footballing ability. They suggested that I needed to work on my first touch, long balls and shooting, which I generally agreed with.

The match at Pride Park was the Derby Under 15s v Derby Under 17s. The under U17s had done as badly as us during the season, so the sides were actually quite evenly matched. The stadium was fantastic, with enough room to hold 33,500 people (although there were less than 100 there to watch us play). They turned the floodlights on too, which made it feel even more special. I played for the under 17s and we drew 2-2.

It was by far the best experience I'd had at the club. When I walked onto the pitch I tried to imagine what it must be like to play in places like this every week in front of 30,000 people. Unfortunately, that could never happen in the women's game. Even in the Super League the biggest clubs play in front of less than 1,000 spectators. At the time, the women's game was a bit odd because there were two top leagues: the Women's Super League (WSL), which was played in the summer, and the Women's Premier League (WPL), which was played in the winter. The WSL has added a second division since then, but there are still only 18 teams in it altogether.

The WSL is definitely the top league, but it's not quite as straightforward as the difference between, say, the Championship and the Premier League. Very few people watch women's football, even at the top level. Attendances for WSL games are increasing, but a lot of tickets are given away for free. There's not the same culture of supporting football among girls as there is with boys. I know some girls who have had season tickets at men's Premier League and Football League clubs (including me), but not many of those watch *Match of the Day* or games on *Sky Sports*.

I don't know anyone else who goes to watch women's football regularly.

I 'support' Sheffield United (the men's team, as there is no official women's team) and I had a season ticket for four years. I enjoyed watching the matches and could see who was doing well and who was doing badly. But unlike Evan, I wasn't interested in learning the name of every single player in the league. And I didn't really follow football on TV. Yet even my lacklustre support for the Blades is not mirrored in the women's game, where I don't really follow any team at all. Again, I don't know anyone who does. It's not the quality of the football that's the problem, as I've been to lots of women's football matches and generally enjoyed them no less than any of the Premier League games I've seen. In fact, the best match I've ever attended was a women's international. It was the semi-final of the 2012 Olympics at Old Trafford between USA and Canada, which finished 4-3 after extra time. I think the problem is that there's just no one to share the experience with.

People say the women's game is slower, but, believe me, WSL matches are a lot faster than any men's game I've ever played in. You've got to be super-fit and able to run and sprint for 90 minutes. The players may not be as fast or as powerful as those I've played against in men's football, but technically they are just as good and, because of the way they play, the game moves a lot quicker. It's a shame more people don't go to watch because the football is really good.

Whenever I had a free Sunday, we used to go to watch matches at two women's clubs: Doncaster Belles, who were in the WSL, and Sheffield FC, who played in the WPL. There was very little to choose between the two in my opinion and both had some fantastic players. Yet despite winning the WPL a few times, Sheffield FC generally played in front of crowds of much less than 100 people, and often even fewer than had turned out to watch my game for Millhouses earlier in the day.

The game at Pride Park was the last of the season. Things hadn't improved for Derby and our last win, against Sheffield United, was a distant memory. The penultimate match, away to Everton, was fairly typical of the run-in. I thought Everton were okay but nothing special. They had a good keeper and were well organised, but lacked the real quality players I'd seen at Blackburn and Manchester United. A six-hour round-trip was punctuated by a 6-0 thumping. I came on halfway through, when we were 4-0 down, and any thoughts of finishing the season on a high had melted away like the Mersey morning mist.

We arrived home at 2:30pm and immediately raced out again to watch Sheffield United lose 1-0 to Leyton Orient. You might think that having the whole day dedicated to disappointing football was a bit depressing, but I was just so happy that I wasn't going to have to face the commute to training again until September. Nothing could dent my mood.

In stark contrast, my return to Millhouses resulted in the most thrilling end to the season I've ever been involved in. With four matches to go, we were in second place, just one point behind the leaders, Thorncliffe Juniors, our next opponents. Our following games were against the other promotion rivals: Brampton in fourth and Brinsworth in third. Our final match was against the bottom club, Maltby. Four wins would see us go up as champions and four points would see us win promotion, but with arguably the three most difficult matches of the season ahead of us, it was nothing like clear cut.

Although we were still winning, despite all the injuries, we had been edging games by the odd goal. We were no longer blowing teams away. Those injuries meant we turned up at Thorncliffe Juniors with just 10 players and no goalkeeper. We got beaten 6-0. It was the first league game we'd lost since September.

We also lost the next match against Brampton, which meant we needed a win and a draw from our last two matches.

We were finally back up to full strength for the game against Brinsworth and went ahead twice, but each time they pulled level. However, a point was enough for both sides so at the final whistle there was the very rare sight of two teams celebrating a draw. If we beat Maltby then we'd be promoted as runners-up. I'll spare you the suspense because there wasn't any. We scored in the first minute and battered them 13-1.

Millhouses might not have been champions, but with all the problems we'd had, runners-up and promotion felt like a real achievement. I'd now be able to look back on my time in boys' football and think, 'Yes, I was good enough to play in the A League'. Playing in the top division is the goal for pretty much every boy who plays football in South Yorkshire. It's a measure of how good you are. When people found out I played for a boys' team, they usually assumed that either the team was rubbish or that I was just making up the numbers.

But if you can say, 'We play in the A League' then people know you must be a good footballer and they take you seriously. This is where all the players from the development squads at Wednesday, Sheffield United and the other professional clubs in the area play. It's also where those boys released by the various academies usually end up. Some of our squad were trying to play it cool, but I could tell that almost everyone was as happy as I was. More excited, in fact, because of course they would all get the chance to play next season... unlike me.

As we'd finished runners-up, we were invited to the 'League Presentation Night' at the grandly named Barnsley Metrodome, which is in fact just a big swimming pool. The champions and runners-up from all seven divisions would be there. When Dad opened the email from Iain giving him details he burst out laughing.

"What's so funny?" asked Mum.

"Listen to this, 'Before the event all the boys will be allowed free use of the swimming pool.' Pack your bikini, Niamh. That's an exclusive invitation to you and around 200 lads!"

I decided to pass on the offer of a free swim, but I was really looking forward to the night. The club had bought us all polo shirts with our initials on. It was quite a warm day so I wore shorts. When I turned up, with my hair down and make-up on (i.e., not in a football kit with my hair tied-up and face covered in mud), it took a few of the team a second to realise it was me.

"Sorry Niamh," said Bilal, "I didn't recognise you. I keep forgetting you're a girl in real life."

"Hey bruv," said Sheriyar without irony. "You've got your shorts on. You don't wanna be wearin' shorts when you go up for your award. You'll get whistles!"

We were on a table all together. I could see a lot of boys from the other teams looking over at us and laughing. As I was wearing the T-shirt they could see I was a player rather than a sister, but they probably assumed I must play for the runners-up in the G League. They were in for a surprise.

The awards took ages. Players were called up individually to get their medals from the League Secretary, and everyone clapped politely as they got their photo taken. Then it was the turn of the runners-up in the G League; then the winners of G; then the runners-up in F... and so on until the overall champions, the winners of A, got their trophy right at the end. Given that each team had a squad of at least 16 players, this took quite some time.

By the time it was our turn to pick up our awards the audience was thoroughly bored. There was a general level of muttering interspersed with a smattering of polite applause every 15 seconds as yet another boy took to the stage to get his trophy. But as Millhouses queued at the side, the muttering started getting a little louder and I could hear a few mums sat nearby ask out loud to no one in particular, "Is that a girl?"

The muttering got much louder when my name was read out, and when I walked on stage the applause was amazing – the loudest of the night. A few people even stood up to clap. I felt very proud – and Sheriyar was right, I did get some whistles!

The final event of the year was our own presentation evening. Things started with a 'Dads v Lads (and Lass)' game, which was good fun (we won of course). After that there was a break before the awards started, so rather than sit and wait we all went to have a look around. Outside the venue, someone noticed there was a massive assault course. If I'd been there with my girl friends we might have wandered over to sit on the swings, but the lads were drawn to it like moths to a light bulb.

They all sprinted towards it as fast as they could, as if there was a chance it might disappear. By the time I got there – perhaps 10 seconds later – a competition had already been organised. I was struck by how lads have to turn every single activity into a competition. For them 'having fun' is not sitting round having a chat, it's got to involve beating someone or trying to prove you're the best at something.

Some of the boys' competitiveness kind of made sense to me, like the assault course for example, where they were trying to see who could climb the highest, who could swing the furthest or who could complete a section the quickest. But a lot of it just baffled me. Getting the best seat in the car seemed almost as important as winning the football match, even if it was just a five-minute ride. Afterwards, back in the venue, food was served and a battle ensued to see who could get the most chips on their plate (from what looked to me like an unlimited supply). This competition dominated the next part of the evening.

"Look at my plate. I'm having loads me," said Dan

What was even stranger to me was that the rest of the team seemed genuinely impressed by his achievement.

"Hey Niamh, you've got hardly any chips," said Munib.

"Well, I don't really want any," I said.

"But you've got to have loads..." he replied, for reasons that never became clear.

Over our chips, Sheriyar asked, "Why are you leaving now Niamh, just as we're goin' into the A League?"

"It's the FA rules, man," said Dan. "Girls can't play no more next season. Niamh's gotta go back to her own kind."

"Hey, why don't you just get your hair cut, make yourself look proper buff like a boy and come and play with us next year?" said Bilal

"How exactly would that work, Billy?" I said.

"It's worth a try, is all I'm saying. If you love our team..."

I wished I could have done that, but after the ceremony was over we said goodbye and that was that. It was sad to think that I probably wouldn't see some of these people again. I thanked Iain for giving me a chance.

"Not at all Niamh, I'd really like to thank you too. I don't think we'd have done it without you. This is a great bunch of players and I'm only sorry you won't be joining us next year. We're going to miss you. We really are."

Dad asked about the plans for next season.

"We've got to get some new players in, but since we've got promoted the phone's not stopped ringing. We've been promoted four years running, but this next league is the biggest step up of all. It should be really interesting."

Like a fairground candy floss, my one season with the boys was over far too quickly. Just as I'd settled in the squad it was time to leave, although I wasn't the only one going. Guido was also leaving – to play basketball for England – but, more surprisingly, so was Dan, although his intentions were a bit more 'sketchy. When I asked him he mumbled something about boxing and wanting to play in midfield.

As we drove home, I thought about what I'd be doing next season. If I stayed at Derby I'd be in the older half of the under 15 age group. Charlotte said I'd find it a lot easier, but I didn't like the sound of that. It wasn't easier I was after. It was better.

Chapter 11

"You Won't be able to Play for England"

"It was great playing with and learning from the boys... I was gutted when I had to leave. It certainly wasn't my choice... I think girls should play football with boys for as long as they possibly can to pick up the pace and resilience you need to succeed in the game."

Casey Stoney, English footballer, former captain of England women

For the first time in my life I was not looking forward to the start of pre-season. During the close season lull from mid-April to the beginning of trials in June, I'm normally climbing the walls after the novelty of a few free weekends has worn off. In previous years I'd fill my time by playing in tournaments for anyone who needed a spare player, but one of the many rules at Derby – and other CoEs – is that you can't play in tournaments, so that particular avenue of fun was now closed. This year, what I was enjoying most of all was not playing football.

I felt guilty for thinking this way so I didn't tell anyone. Charlotte had been trying to be reassuring when she said I'd find it easier next year, but I couldn't help thinking that with all the best players leaving to play at under 17s, that it might be down to the fact that the quality of the opposition wouldn't be as good. Dan and Charlotte had encouraged everyone to try out at other CoEs. You only have your place at a CoE for a year and then everyone has to trial again, "No one's position is guaranteed," they said, adding that it would also be good for us to "experience how things were done elsewhere".

For me, 'elsewhere' meant either Leeds – a 75-minute commute – or Sheffield United. My heart sank even further at the thought of either prospect. In the end I just couldn't face a bigger commute, so Mum contacted Sheffield United – one of only two teams Derby had beaten – to ask about trials. She received an email inviting me down to the CoE at 7pm on 1st June. I pretended to be really pleased at the prospect. At least United were only having one trial: Derby's were spread out over a fortnight.

I thought about going back to playing football for Rovers instead. Derby were probably the slightly better team, and were definitely playing stronger opposition, but there would be a lot less travelling involved for me. It would mean leaving the official 'player pathway' to the WSL or WPL (and England), but it would certainly be a lot more fun for the next few years. Which is what, as people kept reminding me, football was supposed to be about.

We arrived at the Sheffield United training ground 15 minutes early in anticipation of the form-filling that would be required. As well as the forms, we were given a leaflet about the trials, which Dad started to read.

"That's funny. It says here that tonight is the first of four trials. There was no mention of that in the email. I have been thinking it was a bit weird that there was only one."

He turned the leaflet over.

"Ah! Wouldn't you know it? The next two sessions clash with trials at Derby. We'd better tell them that you can't make the other two."

We went into the reception room where three ladies dressed in Sheffield United CoE tracksuits were sitting behind a desk collecting forms. They smiled at us as we walked in.

Aged 6. The goals Nana bought for us were a bit big for the garden.

Aged 7. With my brother Evan (blue bib) at Sheffield Wednesday Soccer Skills.

Getting ready to play football while on holiday in Greece. I'd be wearing the Ireland kit for real eight years later.

(Left) A proud moment – winning the 'Ice Man' for the first time.

(Below) Aged 9. Marking up at a corner during my first season with Sheffield Wednesday.

(Right) On the pitch for a schools tournament at Bramall Lane after I was drafted in from the girls' team.

(Below) Celebrating a third successive league title with Middlewood Rovers

(Top) Millhouses Juniors Under 13 Boys at the end of a hard season.

(Above & right) At the league presentation evening. With all the problems we'd had at Millhouses, runners-up and promotion felt like a real achievement.

(Top left) My final game for Derby at Pride Park. Goodbye Derby County Girls' CoE...

(above) ... Hello Sheffield Wednesday Boys' Elite Player Development Centre. I even had my own changing room!

(left)Millhouses Under 14s with Chris and Bilal. A new kit for our promotion to the A League. (Photo by Shaun Bloodworth)

(Above & right) With Dronfield Town Under 15 Boys at the Stormvogels International Tournament in Amsterdam.

(Below) Captaining South Yorkshire County Under 16 Girls, 2014/15.

(Above) Celebrating with the Ireland squad at St George's Park. We were very happy with our 0-0 draw away to England.

(left) Exhausted after an Ireland game. One hour later, I was on the plane home to make a cup match the following day.

(Above & left) Beighton Magpies
Under 16 Boys, 2015.

(Bottom left & right) Making my
Premier League home debut for
Huddersfield Town against
Coventry in May 2015.

"Hello, this is Niamh and she's come to trial," said Dad.

"Hello Niamh," they said, smiling.

"Unfortunately, there seems to have been a bit of a mix-up. We've only just found out that there are four trials and Niamh will be unable to attend the next two."

"I'm afraid that we need players to attend all trials," said one of the ladies. "That information, and the dates of the trials, were clearly indicated in the email I sent you."

"Actually the email we got only mentioned the trial this evening, but that's not the point..."

"No, it definitely contained all the relevant information."

The lady wasn't smiling anymore. Dad looked a bit confused.

"Honestly it didn't. But anyway the point is that she can't make the other two trials, so we wondered whether the coaches would like to take a look at her tonight and see what they think at the end of the session?"

"I'm sorry, but the coaches will need players to attend all the sessions before they make their assessment. As was clearly stated in the email I sent you."

"Okay, just so I'm clear – what you're saying is there's absolutely no point in Niamh trying out this evening?"

The lady smiled again, but didn't look quite as friendly.

"No, I'm afraid there isn't."

She turned to me.

"Unless you'd like to take part for a bit of extra training and the experience of actually playing at a Centre of Excellence."

If I'm honest, I didn't think that I did want to take part in a bit of extra training and the experience of actually playing at a Centre of Excellence.

"No, thank you," I said as politely as possible. "Can we just go, Dad?"

"Okay thanks for the offer, but I think we'll leave it," said Dad.

As we were about to go, one of the other ladies, who had

been silent up until then said, "You do realise that if you don't come to a Centre of Excellence you won't be able to play for England, don't you?"

Dad turned round. He'd gone a bit red in the face and looked like he was going to say something in a loud voice that might involve swearing. I was praying that he wouldn't.

"Thanks for being so helpful," he said calmly.

Luckily the ladies didn't seem to notice he was being sarcastic. We walked back to the car in silence. On the drive home Dad said quite a few things that I couldn't possibly write down.

The first week of trials at Derby was just training. In the first session all we did was run around and do some passing drills. Anyone can turn up to trial at a CoE, but if this was intended to entice the local elite from grassroots, on this evidence it didn't seem to be working. Only one of my former teammates at Rovers – County Cup and League winners for the fourth year running – went for a trial at a CoE. And that was because she was always on the bench and unhappy with the little amount of pitch time she was receiving. Fair play to her for trying though, because she did get in.

There were trialists at Derby who had obviously never even played for a team before. A couple of girls turned up with neither boots nor shin pads. There were no surprises when the call-backs for the second week were announced. It looked like the squad was going to be roughly as strong as it had been the previous season.

On the way home from the second trial, I broke some news.

"Dad, I don't think I want to play for Derby anymore."

"Are you sure? You need to think about that. Why don't you see how you feel at the trials and make your decision then?"

"Because I don't want to play for them. Everyone's really nice and I'm sure it's brilliant and I know it's a privilege, but it's just not for me. I think I might just pack it in and do something else."

"Look, I would never make you do something you don't want to do, so if you don't want to go to Derby, don't go to Derby. But you don't really want to give football up, do you?"

"No, not really. I just don't think there's an alternative."

"I'll look into what the options are tomorrow. I'll try the FA again and there's a guy I used to work with who's a football coach. I think he's working at Sheffield Wednesday, but he used to coach in the women's game. I'll give him a call."

I tried to be positive, but it didn't sound very hopeful. I thought I might just go back to play for Rovers and take up athletics instead.

The next day I was walking through the park with my friends on my way home from school when I got a text. It was from Dad and said: 'The FA has just announced that they are extending the age limit for girls to play with boys to under 14s. Do you want me to give Iain a ring?' I was so happy and I texted right back: 'Yes!' I was so excited, I started jumping and cheering. My friends were looking really confused, and even more so when I tried to explain to them what had happened.

People assume it was a difficult decision to leave Derby, but it wasn't. I didn't feel that I was choosing between boys and girls either. I just wanted to play for the best team I could at the highest possible standard. Millhouses were a better team than Derby and they were going to be playing against better teams. I thought I'd improve more and enjoy it more. It was as simple as that really. There was also the bonus that I wouldn't have to spend seven or eight hours travelling every week.

Dad told Dan I wouldn't be coming. He was okay about it and said he'd be very happy to see me at trials the following year if there was no further rule change. That was pretty decent of him I think.

When I turned up for the first trials at Millhouses the boys looked just as surprised as they had the previous year (I guessed that the FA's announcement about mixed football hadn't come up on their radar), but they seemed quite happy that I was coming back. However, there was another shock that was not so good. Iain announced that he was stepping down as manager for personal reasons. He was still going to be involved, but the team was now going to be run exclusively by Dave. I was very sad to hear this. I liked Iain and thought he was a good manager. He used to be a vicar, but you'd never have guessed that if you heard him shouting from the touchline. At least he wasn't disappearing altogether.

As we started warming up, it was clear that there were a huge number of trialists. All of them had played for other teams and all of them had their own boots and shin pads.

In fact, the quality was really impressive. Quite a few lads had come from teams relegated from the A League, while others were kids who'd won player of the season or been top goalscorer at clubs from lower divisions. There were also a couple of boys who'd been released by the Sheffield Wednesday and Sheffield United academies. It might have only been a trial match, but with so much competition and so many players trying to prove something, it wasn't like playing in a friendly.

As the game went on two outstanding players emerged. One was a midfielder called Dexter, who'd had a few seasons at Sheffield Wednesday's academy. The other was a 6ft tall, insanely fast, two-footed striker called Josh. Unfortunately for me, Josh was playing on the left wing. I got a really good challenge in early on which settled my nerves, but he was a real handful. The previous season he had been the top scorer in the Huddersfield Junior League and I was finding out why.

He kept skinning me, which was infuriating, but made me hope that we signed him. One time Josh received the ball from a corner, but rather than hit it first time he took a touch, so I slid in and won the ball just as he was about to pull the trigger. It knocked him right off his feet, and was made all the more spectacular because he was so tall. It was like watching a tent collapse. At the end of the game a few people were given a registration form. I was very pleased to be among them and was also happy to see Dexter and Josh being handed one each as well.

There were even more players for the second trial. Afterwards Dave announced that, in light of being so short the previous season, he was going to be signing 16 players. I was glad to be already one of the squad, but 16 seemed like too many. Dave also had a very different management style to Iain. He was more stick than carrot and consequently not as popular with the players, although that isn't necessarily a problem if the players respect you.

Throughout my first season at Millhouses I kept getting asked why I didn't play for the school team. I had played for the girls' team before, but girls' football in schools is a bit of a joke. Only three other girls in my year actually played for a team. The rest of the side had never played football before. I always thought our matches must look like what Andy Gray or Richard Keys imagined all women's football to be like. The games were awful, with bunches of players from both teams running after the ball and hoofing it. There was no point passing, you might as well try and dribble up the pitch and take a shot. I scored nine goals in one game. That's not really football at all, so I gave it up.

Our coach was the P.E teacher, Miss Giampalma. She was actually a footballer herself, and a very good one. A fast and skilful winger, she played for Sheffield FC and had a couple of Premier League winners medals. I'd watched her play quite a few times and had been really impressed. However, I think I went down in her estimation when I said I didn't want to play for the girls' football team any more. I tried to explain why, but she made me feel like I was being big-headed, which certainly wasn't the case, and I was left with the feeling that I'd disappointed her.

What I really wanted to do was play for the boys' team. The year before, when the mixed football rule changed, I had asked the boys' coach, Mr O'Sullivan, if I could try out again. He said I couldn't because the rules hadn't changed for school teams. I later found out that he'd made a mistake and that the rule also applied to schools' football. The following year I decided to try once more. After playing with Millhouses for a year I was a lot more confident. I knew quite a few lads who played for the school and had come up against some of them in the league, so I knew I was good enough to be considered.

I tracked down Mr O'Sullivan and asked him if I could take part in the trials. Before he had a chance to fob me off again, I explained to him that I'd checked with the FA and I was definitely allowed to play. Mr O'Sullivan had never taught me, so he didn't know who I was or anything about me, and I imagine he probably thought I was just wasting his time. That might have explained the strange look on his face, as if he was thinking, 'In God's name, which madman sanctioned that crazy idea?' But what he actually said was, "Erm, okay then. Trials are at lunchtime this Friday."

The trials took place on the school's 3G pitch. There is seating down one side, but usually there aren't that many spectators for the Year 9 trial. There might be a few lads from older years who've come down to mock the 'little kids' but that's pretty much it. Today was different though.

Lunchtimes at school can be pretty boring, so once word got round that a girl was going to be trying out for the Year 9 team a load of people decided to come along and watch.

I'm not stupid. Most of them had come along in the hope of witnessing some lunchtime comedy. They couldn't lose: if I played badly, they'd be able to laugh at how rubbish I was; but if I played well, it would be the lads I was up against they'd be laughing at. I was determined to make sure there was plenty to laugh at for the right reasons. As soon as I ran out onto the pitch there was a huge cheer from the large crowd. Of course they weren't really cheering me on, they were doing it to wind up the other players, but cheers are cheers – you take what you can get.

Mr O'Sullivan split us into four teams and set up two games. Once it became clear which game I was playing in, all the spectators moved down to that end of the pitch. There was no one watching the other game. They'd sit pretty much in silence until it looked like I was going to get on the ball, at which point they'd start revving up. Every time I did get on the ball or made a pass, they'd make as much noise as possible. They loved it whenever I made a tackle and they'd jeer at the player I'd won the ball from for ages afterwards. But the first time I headed the ball back from the keeper's kick out there were a few gasps of amazement. I think some of the other players found it off-putting, but I thought it was really funny. It just made me want to play better and tackle harder. The standard in our game was nowhere near what I was used to on Sundays. It was much slower, so I had a lot more time on the ball. I could run with it and think about the next pass. I never felt under too much pressure. Lads in the crowd kept telling me to get forwards and shoot. I just played my usual game, but it would have been funny to see the reaction if I had actually scored.

There was, unfortunately, one important person not watching our game. Mr O'Sullivan spent almost the whole time involved with the match on the other pitch. He did come over to us for the last 15 minutes, but I spent most of that time in nets. As we walked off the pitch and I headed back to the girls' changing room, a few lads from the school team said they thought I'd played really well and would probably get in the team. It was good to hear – I knew it wasn't something they'd just say – but I was a lot less confident about my chances.

Sure enough, a few days later the team was posted up on the noticeboard and I wasn't in it. I knew the boy who'd got in ahead of me quite well. He'd been to my junior school and played Sunday football for a team in one of the bottom leagues. I'm not saying I was definitely better than him, but I didn't feel like I'd been beaten by the better player. That evening I told my dad what had happened.

"It's not like we haven't been here before, is it?" he said. "I am very disappointed for you though, and all I can say is that they must have a very good school team if you didn't get in."

Dad also said that there was no point making a fuss as Mr O'Sullivan would just say he could only go on what he saw and that other people appeared better.

"If you like though, I can write to the P.E department and get some feedback from them. At least you'll know exactly why you didn't get in."

I thought that that was a good idea.

Around this time I started to notice a not-so-subtle change in my girl friends. None of them had ever been bothered about football before, but now they started hatching plans to sleep over at my house and come and watch me (or rather, boys they fancied) play in the morning. These plans rarely amounted to much, but at least they were finally taking an interest.

I also got the impression that my team-mates at Millhouses loved it when my friends came to watch. We trained on the

3G at a local school. Quite a few local teams trained there and, one time, on the pitch next to us were Sheffield FC Under 15 Girls. They were girls from the year above. Older girls. The best kind. I recognised a couple of their players and said 'hello' as they walked past. Behind me I could hear Bilal and some of the other the lads talking about them.

"Hey man, check her out. Look at that!" said Bilal.

'What!?' I thought. I think they'd forgotten I was there.

"So Billy, what exactly are you checking out?" I said.

"Nothing, man. I just meant check her boots out, man. She's got right nice boots on. Nice boots. That's all."

"Yeah Niamh, chill out," said Joel. "We've got total respect for women haven't we... especially ones that look like her."

I recognised two more girls from the Sheffield United development squad. They were twins. Again I said 'hello'.

"Oh man, how come you know all the fittest girls, Niamh? Can you introduce me to either of them? Or both of them?"

"I wouldn't want to waste your time, Billy," I said.

Another time I was warming up before a game one Sunday afternoon and bumped into one of my friends who was out walking her dog. She stopped and chatted for a while, asking me what I was doing, making conversation. While we were talking, I could feel the boys' eyes burrowing into the back of my head, exactly like they would have been if one of them was caught *talking to a girl!*

After she'd gone I went back into the warm-up.

"How do you know her?" asked Luke.

"We do dancing together on Saturday afternoons," I said.

Luke couldn't get his breath.

"You do *dancing?*"

I could see he was revving up to take the mickey big time, like he'd unearthed a rich vein of comedy.

"You actually DO *dancing*, Niamh?"

"Calm down, Luke. Remember, I am actually a girl. Girls do dancing."

He looked deflated, like I'd just proven to him that there was no Santa.

"Oh yeah," he said. "But still. You doing dancing! I just can't imagine it."

While the football in the A League was a great standard, there was an atmosphere at matches that I didn't like. It seemed to start on the touchline and spill onto the pitch. Apart from us, who hardly anyone came to watch, the teams seemed to have a lot more spectators, who generally took the game very seriously. And not necessarily in a good way.

I don't know why more people came to watch. Maybe just because the football was better, or maybe they thought their lad still had a chance of making it. Whatever the reason the bigger crowds didn't make for a better atmosphere. Parents were often more vocal and would react badly to refereeing decisions against their team. I've even heard of parents fighting, although I've never seen that. A good example of this was our biggest game of the season, against Handsworth.

Handsworth were not only reigning A League champions and County Cup holders, but they'd only lost one game in three years. This season they looked unbeatable, averaging five goals a game in a very good league. All the best players gravitated towards Handsworth. Over the years, if they regularly lost players to one of the academies, then they usually picked up the ones coming out. I was really looking forward to playing them.

We were at home, which meant a long walk from the car park up the hill. I could see that Handsworth had arrived early and were already warming up. I was relieved to see that they were normal sized, as you really do build teams like that up to be giants in your head.

They had a lot of supporters. One family had brought camping chairs to take the weight off their feet. They were sat near one of the goals and we had to walk past them as we arrived. I could see them staring at me all the way up the hill. As we got nearer I could hear them talking about me too.

"I told you it was a girl," said a lady in a big coat to a man sat beside her. He started shaking his head.

"Bloody ridiculous!" he replied, and rolled his eyes.

"I know. She just won't be strong enough, will she?"

"We can hear you, you know," said Dad, smiling at them.

They lowered their voices after that, but I could see they were still talking about me.

"Don't ignore them, Niamh,' said Dad. "Use it to get yourself fired up. They don't look like they've played much football to me. Surprise them."

It wasn't just me the Handsworth supporters had a problem with. During the game one man kept asking Bilal and Sheriyar whether they were going to be driving their taxis home. Someone asked him to stop, but he told them to "give over" and said it was "just banter".

One of the other spectators said, "Come on, they're just kids."

"You're joking, aren't you?" said the man pointing at Bilal. "He's at least 20."

It certainly put Billy off his game, but it also had an effect on their players too, who were constantly having a go at the referee. We had a few on our team like that – every team does – but that day felt like their entire side was at it.

At one point the keeper picked up a loose ball, but instead of getting on with the game he used the fact he was now the centre of attention as an opportunity to scream at the referee about an earlier decision. The ref booked him. Some of their supporters weren't happy about that.

Late in the second half I fouled the left-winger in the corner. I went for the ball, but he skilled me and I caught him instead. It was a late challenge and was definitely a free kick.

The winger was rolling around on the floor holding his ankle. His team's supporters started shouting for the referee to book me. I overheard someone saying I was "an effing disgrace". I tried to ignore them. The referee gave the free kick, but some people still wanted to see a booking. The ref called me over.

"I tried to get the ball, but he really was to quick for me," I said. "I didn't mean it."

"I know you didn't," said the ref, "but just be careful. You were late."

No booking. Outrage on the touchline.

I tried shaking the kid's hand but he just slapped it away. There's a lot of talk about bad losers, but this was the first time I'd experienced a bad winner. We lost 4-0 and were never really in the match.

On the way back to the car park we saw the large man waiting by his car. He watched as we walked down the hill and came over to talk to us.

'Excuse me," he said to Dad, "but could you please explain to me what that booking was for?"

Dad had been running the line and was responsible for Millhouses' admin, so I think the guy might have thought he had something to do with the referee. I think he was referring to their goalkeeper, or he might have meant, 'Why wasn't she booked?' Either way, he wasn't being friendly.

"If you don't know why he was booked, then I don't think anything I can say to you is going to help you," said Dad.

"What do you mean?" said the man, quite aggressively.

"I'm sorry," said Dad, "but I think you've mistaken me for someone who cares. If you've got a problem with the ref you should take it up with the league, not me."

We walked past but the man didn't seem like he wanted the conversation to end there. He carried on shouting at us as we walked to the car. I thought Dad was going to turn round and say something else, but thankfully he didn't.

I was still enjoying the football, but was disappointed that our team seemed to be underperforming. We had some of the best players in the league, but weren't winning many games. I think it was because we went into matches underprepared. Unlike a lot of the other A League clubs, we trained only once a week for an hour and it wasn't enough. While most teams in the league were set up to play to a system with tactics, we weren't. Rather than pass the ball to each other, our midfield tended to try and run with it instead. They were usually skilful enough to beat the first man, but not a second or third. We also played the same formation every week, no matter what. This made us too predictable.

Strangely, some of the season's lowlights were actually highlights. In a game against Staveley we managed to score early in the game, but then spent the rest of the first half hanging on. Staveley battered away at us but just couldn't score. With a couple of minutes to go before half time they won a corner. I was on the front post. From the cross, the ball was headed above me towards the top corner of the goal. I jumped but there was no way I could get high enough to head it so, instinctively, I put my hand up and punched it clear. I didn't mean to cheat; I didn't think about doing it, it just seemed to happen. But it was deliberate handball and I'd prevented a certain goal, so it should have been a penalty, a straight red card and a one-match ban.

The Staveley players, the subs and coaches on the bench, and all their parents on the touchline started screaming for a penalty. I didn't hear the referee's whistle and managed to get to the ball and boot it out for a throw-in. Still I waited for the whistle, but the ref was waving the players away and signaling for a throw-in. The team surrounded him demanding that he change his decision because, "That girl just handballed it deliberately!" But it was no use. He was the only person who hadn't seen it. My heart was pounding. I said to myself, 'If he asks me, I'll admit it', but he didn't.

Getting nowhere with the ref, some of the players turned on me. "You effing cheat!" one of them said.

I admit he had a point, but he did look like he wanted to kill me. The referee gave him a warning for that. The next time I got the ball there was a late challenge. I played the ball down the line and the player slid in about a second later. There was no attempt to play the ball. A few minutes later, the same thing happened, but this time it was a different player. I managed to get out of the way, but it was still a free kick for dangerous play. The ref said that the next late challenge would get a booking. When the ref blew for half time he was surrounded by the Staveley coaches. It was an understatement to say that not giving the handball had been a controversial decision.

Dave looked at me as I walked over.

"I can't condone it Niamh, but you have actually kept us in the game."

"I do feel a bit bad about it but I think they're going to kill me," I said.

"Shall I ask Alitaker if he fancies a run-out?"

"I think that's probably a good idea."

The rest of the team were, however, delighted with the result of my handball. In all the time I was at Millhouses, I don't think I was every congratulated as much for anything else. While I was warming down I apologised to the Staveley manager and explained it was an instinctive reaction.

"No hard feelings at all, love. We all do what we can, don't we? It's the referee I'm annoyed with for not seeing it."

We shook hands. I'm not proud of it but that handball was to prove pretty important at the end of the season.

That was the final game before the Christmas break, so Dave and Iain arranged to take us all ice skating for our Christmas party. I'd been skating before, but only with my friends, and I wasn't totally sure about going. I thought my team-mates might just be really laddy and wouldn't want me tagging along, but it was free and I like ice skating, so I went along.

Iain picked me up. I was the last one into the car and Bilal had 'won' the front seat and was eating a kebab, which the others complained was stinking the place out. In the back I had plenty of room as Sheriyar did his best to avoid any physical contact. Meanwhile, Finn on his other side was moaning about being squashed into the car door.

Bilal finished his kebab and started texting girls from his school. He held up a photo of one to the boys, making sure I couldn't see it.

"Hey Sherry, doesn't that look like Niamh?"

Who knows what it really was a photo of, but Sherry and Finn thought it was hilarious. I rolled my eyes in anticipation of a long evening.

At the ice rink, we went to collect our boots. There were two kinds: white figure skating boots or black ice hockey boots. I could see where this was heading so I was relieved when I was allocated a pair of ice hockey books. Poor Sheriyar was less fortunate.

"Hey everyone! Look at Sherry. He's got girls' boots on!" someone shouted.

Now, given he had no say in the matter, you would think the obvious response to that would be "And?" But you'd be wrong. The lads couldn't have laughed more if Sheriyar had turned up for training in a tutu.

I'd always found ice skating to be a fairly low-key exercise. Once you've got the hang of it, whizzing round in a big circle doesn't take much effort. This evening though, it was competition time: who could go the fastest forwards/backwards/in a figure of eight/straight line/relays. When the novelty of that wore off they decided they would all try and pull some girls. At this point, I took on a newfound usefulness.

"Niamh, will you talk to this girl for me..."

"Niamh, can you talk to that girl for me..."

"Niamh, can you please ask that girl if..."

"Hey Niamh, can you go over to that girl there please and tell her how great I am," asked Bilal.

"I don't think I can to do that Billy. I already spoke to her for Sherry and he's with her now."

They were rushing round, showing off in front of the girls, knocking each other into the wall and laughing like drains if anyone fell over (how unexpected on an ice rink), so I decided to take myself off for a quiet skate on my own. I'd done a few laps when a boy came over to skate alongside me and he kept looking across and smiling. After a lap or two of this, he turned so he was skating backwards (skills!), smiled again, and said, "Hi! What's your name?"

Before I had a chance to answer, his expression changed to one of alarm and he turned and skated off as quickly as possible. I looked behind me to see what had startled him. It was the whole of the Millhouses team skating towards me as fast as they could.

"Was that kid bothering you?" said Bilal, as five or six other lads crashed into me. "I'll get you fixed up with someone better than that. Which one of us do you fancy? I reckon it's James. There must be one of us."

"You might be surprised to hear that I don't think about you in that way," I replied. "Perhaps it's because I know you too well."

Now that was definitely true.

Our pre-season target had been to avoid relegation. But while that had looked easily achievable at Christmas, now with just three games to go it seemed almost impossible. Dave stuck rigidly to the same formation and tactics whatever happened. In one game, which I started on the bench, we were 4-0 down in 10 minutes. Our tactical response was to change the left-midfielder three times. We went on to lose 6-1.

Our next match was the return fixture against Handsworth. They'd won every single game and only needed a draw to secure the title. They had shifted the kick-off to a Thursday so they could clinch the league under floodlights, playing on the senior team's non-league ground. It did make it feel like a really special match, even if we thought we had hardly any chance of winning.

After the warm-up Dave did something revolutionary: he changed the formation. Instead of the 4-4-2 we'd played all season, he switched to 5-4-1. He left Bilal up front on his own, playing Alex as a sweeper and rotating Sheriyar and me with James and Alitaker as wing-backs. It was a remarkable game and we won. The final score, 3-0, makes it sound like we cruised to victory, but Dad said it was the most one-sided 3-0 he'd ever seen. Handsworth had all the possession, but we restricted them to long shots and at half time it was still 0-0. The second half panned out much the same as the first, but as time and the pressure piled on, they pushed further forwards. We scored our first with 15 minutes to go. Just a big boot over the top, which caught out their centre-back for the first time, and Bilal did his thing and ran up the pitch and scored.

They immediately started arguing amongst themselves and were still bickering when they kicked off. Bilal ran in, won the ball and continued running past the midfield (I don't think I ever saw him pass it). He was brought down in the box by a defender. Josh never missed a penalty, so suddenly it was 2-0. I still thought they were going to win. It got really nasty and challenges were late. Sheriyar got flattened and I got called an "effing slag" for booting the ball into row Z when I could have tapped it out for a throw. But we hung on and in the last minute Bilal broke away again and scored a third. At the final whistle we reacted like we'd won the league, while

Handsworth looked like they'd been robbed of the World Cup. Some called us cheats, some started crying and most refused to shake hands (which just made me laugh).

"Ah, don't cry," I said to the kid who'd called me a slag and was now refusing to shake hands.

"F*** off," he barked through the tears.

'So much for your three-year unbeaten record!' I thought.

Dave went up in my estimation after that result. We'd shown what a good team we could be and how, with the right tactics, we could be a match for anyone... but then he changed back to 4-4-2 for the next game and we lost 3-1.

Chapter 12
Trying to Get Better

"Let's not make it a gender issue. Let's talk about football, not whether someone's male or female."
Hope Powell, former England Women's team manager

Dad had a reply from Miss Nicholls, the head of the school P.E department, about my unsuccessful trial for the boys' school team.

Dear Mr McKevitt,

Thank you for your patience in waiting for my reply. I have now spoken again to the teachers who were at the trials and who are still of the opinion that Niamh is not 'strong enough' to play in this particular team.

She also added:

Niamh has the chance to play for the school in the girls' squad, which Miss Giampalma will coach.

Regards,
Miss Nicholls

I was disappointed with this response. There were deficiencies in my game, but this was the first time I'd been criticised for not being strong enough.

I thought it was probably best to just forget about school

football altogether, but I asked Miss Giampalma if she'd be willing to put me up for a trial with the South Yorkshire County girls' under 16 team. I knew the county had a side, but had no idea how you could get into it. I thought it would be a very high standard, but felt that I might be in with a chance. A few days later I got an email from her to say that trials for the under 16s team were being held at the end of September and she'd put my name forward.

I'd been thinking about where I was going to play when I was older as I knew the FA would stop raising the age limit for mixed football at some point. I'd watched the film *Bend it Like Beckham*, at the end of which two girls win scholarships to play football at university in America. This sounded fantastic to me and Dad confirmed that college scholarships did exist for the best athletes. We checked online to see what I needed to do. It said the minimum requirement was usually to have played at academy or regional (County) level. I'd just left an academy, but if I could get into the County squad then that wouldn't matter.

It also made me think about how I could get better. Despite our shortcomings, Millhouses were definitely a better team than Derby and the A League was a much higher standard than the CoE under 15s had been. The problem was the coaching I was missing. At Derby I'd been training four hours a week and learning how to become a better player from very good UEFA-qualified coaches. Dave did his best, but with just an hour a week there wasn't time to do anything really. If only I could have combined the two.

Dad agreed that I needed extra coaching. He contacted an old friend of his, Richard Stevenson, who was one of the goalkeeping coaches at Sheffield Wednesday, to see if he could recommend anything. A few days later Dad announced: "I have some good news. Richard's currently working at Wednesday's Elite Player Development Centre. I talked to him about you and he said, 'Bring Niamh down on Saturday morning. She can train with our lads and we'll have a look at her.'"

We met Richard outside the training ground. He was really friendly. He told us about the EPDC and said it was a bridge between grassroots and academies.

"What we do is take boys who've been dropped from the academies round here – not just Wednesday, but the likes of United, Chesterfield, Barnsley, Rotherham – and put them through a three-month training programme with a view to sending them back out for trials."

"With Wednesday?" Dad asked.

"Because we're affiliated to Wednesday, they get first refusal, but we've got kids going all over. We've got one lad out at Liverpool for six weeks at the moment. Others are at Doncaster, Mansfield, United."

"And do they get in?" I asked.

"Yeah, a lot of them do. The training here is nothing like you've experienced before at Derby or Sheffield United, Niamh. At Derby they will have run the FA programme. A lot of people question whether it's working – it changes every year. We use a Dutch system called 'Coerver'. It's completely different, based on individual skills and ball control, and drills are designed to replicate real game situations. In theory everything you learn here you should be able to take into your matches.

"Coerver's big in Holland, where it came from. The French FA use it and so do Bayern Munich, Arsenal and Newcastle. I promise you won't believe the improvement it will make. We've had kids come here with very little idea and leaving 12 weeks later, looking like world-beaters."

It sounded good to me. I'd always been very confident when it comes to stopping people play and I'm pretty good in the air, but I wasn't particularly creative and my first touch was my biggest weakness.

The sessions lasted two hours and were split into two parts.

The first part was open to anyone, but there were no other girls there. In this session we were all given a ball and the head coach, Gavin, stood in the middle and showed us a skill drill that we had to complete – maybe a stepover, drag-back or turn. Then we'd get into pairs and have to put them together in combination. Nobody seemed to take any notice of me, which was good. I think that's because most of these drills were done in ones or twos and Gavin told you who you were pairing up with. He didn't like people partnering up with their mates, which is a good way to avoid cliques developing.

Richard was right, it was nothing like Derby training. It must have been an impressive sight for anyone watching: 70 kids all doing exactly the same drill at exactly the same time.

For the second session we were split into groups. I was put into 'Elite Under 14' (I have to admit, I quite liked the sound of that). I recognised quite a few of the lads in our group from the A League, so we nodded and said "Alright" to each other. I immediately felt quite relaxed. I'd still have to play my best, but it wasn't like these guys hadn't seen me play before. They knew who I was, which team I played for and what kind of player I was, just as I knew all about them. For example, I knew that Tommy was a winger with quick feet who played for Brinsworth, passed the ball well and had a good shot on him.

This session was all about putting the things we'd learned into small-sided matches. It was really technical. Before the game the coaches told us what runs we were expected to make whenever the ball was in a certain area of the pitch and there was a shape we had to adopt when we had the ball, and another when we were defending. I was working with lads who were either preparing for professional club trials, or already undergoing them. One kid, Masai, was halfway through a six-week trial with Liverpool. During the game the coaches talked all the time, regularly stopping play to tell us when something was being done well or when we were getting things wrong.

I was playing centre-back and Richard was our coach. He was fantastic. His instructions were really clear and his advice really made sense. He was also brilliant at reading the game and identifying problems really quickly.

At one point the goalkeeper rolled the ball out to me. I looked to pass it out to the right but there was nothing on so I tried to turn to go to the left. That gave the striker enough time to close me down and I panicked, tried to go long and ended up whacking the ball into him and losing possession. Richard immediately stopped the game and I thought, 'Oh crap! This is going to be really embarrassing. *The girl* is going to get a bollocking'.

But instead Richard turned to the right-back, who was halfway up the pitch.

"What on earth are you doing there?" he asked.

The lad shrugged.

"Dunno."

"Where should you be standing?"

The lad pointed towards our touchline.

"Down there."

"Down there. That's right, down there. So why did she give the ball away?"

"Because I was standing in the wrong position."

"Right again. She looked for you and you weren't there. If this was a game that could have cost us a goal. And I'd now be taking you off. Play on!"

I thought about how many times I'd seen a player give the ball away in a professional match by either holding on to it for too long or passing it, seemingly without thinking, into an empty space. The crowd would usually respond by booing them. I now realised that it wasn't always their fault, but that of whichever player failed to make the right run and wasn't where he was supposed to be.

At the end of the session Richard came with me to find Dad.

"Right I've spoken to Gav and we'll have her. You're a good player, read the game well and can take instruction. I think you'll benefit from coming here. We'll work on that touch. You won't believe the difference in a few weeks. We've got Leicester this afternoon if you can make it."

"What? You play matches?" I said.

This was brilliant news. I thought it was just coaching.

"Yeah. We try to play at least two a month, on Saturdays so it doesn't interfere with your club games. Usually we play against academy teams or development squads. It's Leicester Academy today, but if you can't make that we've got another match in a fortnight against Derby County Academy Development – the boys' team. I'll put you in the squad for that one if you like."

"I didn't think girls were allowed to play for boys' academies."

"You're right, you can't. But you can play for us *against* them. We're not an academy. If the FA says girls can play at under 14, you can play for our under 14 team. If you want to."

I did.

Getting a place at the EPDC also made me more confident about the South Yorkshire County trial. When I turned up they ticked my name off a register and asked me what school I went to and whether I was in Year 10 or Year 11.

"I'm at Notre Dame and I'm in Year 9," I said.

There were 22 girls there. The coaches split us into two teams and played a practice match. It was one of those occasions when I knew I was playing well. I felt like I was going to win every tackle and header; that every pass would go to one of our players. After the game the coaches read out the names of the players who'd been successful and I'd made the cut. Yes!

But just as the news was sinking in, a man came over and asked if he could speak to Niamh McKevitt. He said he needed to talk to me and asked my dad to join us. He took us to one side.

"Hi, I'm Pete Harper, the manager of the South Yorkshire under 16s. Unfortunately I'm the bearer of some really bad news. I've spent the past 35 minutes on the phone trying to find a way around this issue, but I'm afraid there just isn't one.

"Our insurance only covers girls in Year 10 and Year 11. I've rung the insurers to see if they'll make an exception, but they simply will not let us put a Year 9 girl on the insurance. I've also contacted the FA and they said that girls are only allowed to play a year up. As Niamh would effectively be playing two years up, she's ineligible this season."

I started to cry. I couldn't help it.

"I did wonder," said Dad. "I know in grassroots you can't play two years up, but I assumed this was a case of, 'if you're good enough, you're old enough.'"

"I know where you're coming from," said Pete. "But whether I agree with you or not, there's simply nothing we can do. It'll be regarded as a health and safety issue by the powers that be. I'm sorry.

"The only thing I will say is that we have now seen Niamh and know what a good player she is, which will put her in good stead for the trials next year."

Pete was being really nice. I could see it wasn't his fault. In fact it didn't seem to be anybody's fault, but it just felt so unfair.

I think I improved more as a player during my time at the EPDC than anywhere else. I've never settled into a team quicker. The lads that knew me from the A League were cool about having me in the team, while those that didn't know me simply followed their example. The first game against Derby was the most technical I'd ever played in. It was a bit like the Derby CoE but, without being mean, with better players. I played centre-back. The other centre-back was a guy called Warren who already had a scholarship at Sheffield Wednesday. (Warren went on to play for Manchester United Under 16s in the World Championship a few seasons later.)

If the reaction of our players to my inclusion in the squad was relaxed, Derby's reaction to our entire team was one of total surprise. This time it wasn't just me either. Our players were all really good, but I couldn't help noticing how small they were. Apart from Warren I was the tallest on the team by some distance. On the other hand, Derby were massive. They must have thought they had been put against an under 11 side by mistake. I heard one kid say, "Look at the size of them! And is that a girl?"

It tells you something about how small our team was that he noticed our height before he noticed me. They must have thought it was a wasted journey: 'Who are we playing today? A load of little kids and a girl! Wednesday are in trouble.' But we weren't.

Before the game I had my first, and to date only ever, changing room situation. The Wednesday kit was handed out before the game. All the lads went into the 'Home Team' changing room, Derby went into the 'Away Team' changing room and I went into 'Niamh's Changing Room': I had the entire place to myself. Once I'd changed, I waited outside the Wednesday changing room while Dad checked everyone was decent, then I went in for the team talk.

Gavin and Richard went through how they wanted each of us to play. It was really technical and there was a lot to remember, but it paid off in the match. The golden rule was to always give the player on the ball two options. It all depended on being in the right position so that when you were on the ball yourself, you didn't really need to do much more than remember where you were supposed to pass it. The system worked really well. We passed it around really quickly and, eventually, Derby would get pulled out of shape. They never got to use their advantages of size and strength, because they couldn't get the ball off us. We ended up winning 5-0. I could see that Derby looked a bit shellshocked after the game, as if they couldn't quite believe what had happened.

Millhouses avoided relegation. I'd enjoyed the season; it had been tough, but given that getting into the A League had been the aim last year, managing to stay in it this year also felt like an achievement. I felt I'd proved to myself that I could hold my own at this level. Despite all that, I also felt it was time to move on from Millhouses and play somewhere else. I'd really enjoyed playing for Iain, but I didn't rate Dave as highly. We'd underperformed in my mind. He was a nice guy, but I wanted to find a different team.

There was still no news from the FA about extending the mixed football rule to under 15, so once again I was faced with the uncertainty over where I would be playing next year. This year I decided not to do anything too hasty. By now we had worked out that the decision would be taken at the FA shareholders' AGM at the end of May, so we knew when to look out for an announcement.

My final event with Millhouses was the club's annual presentation evening. Dave made a speech about each of the players before giving them an award and then picked a player of the year. He said some kind things about me, describing me as the hardest tackler in the team (which I liked) and said how difficult it must be for me to compete being a girl (which I didn't like so much). It was no more difficult for me to compete than anyone else. I'm never bothered when someone refers to the team collectively as 'lads' or 'boys' or says I've been 'Man of the Match' because it just means I'm being taken seriously as a player.

The highlight of the evening for me was when Iain, our old manager, said he had a good story to tell. A few days earlier the League Secretary had contacted him and asked, "You haven't got a girl playing for you, have you?"

When Iain said that he had, the secretary replied, "Thank goodness for that. We've been looking for her for weeks. I can't believe we've finally found her."

He explained that the FA was conducting further research into the success of its mixed football policy and had asked the leagues with girls in them to report how we were getting on. Initially our league didn't think they had any girls playing, but the FA said they'd had an email from a parent whose daughter played in the under 14 league (which must have been Dad).

And the reason they couldn't find me? They never thought to look in the A League! They never imagined that a girl would be good enough to play in the top division, so they began their search at the clubs in the bottom division. Their assumption was that if there really was a girl playing, this was probably where they'd find her.

Over the next few weeks a few managers confirmed that they knew of a girl 'playing somewhere' and there were even a few confirmed sightings, but they still couldn't track me down. And so they climbed through every division, from G to B, contacting over 60 teams without any luck. Eventually, they had to check the A League, just to make sure, and the first manager they rang had said, "Yes there is, and she plays for Millhouses."

That story made me happier than winning any award.

I didn't tell the lads I was leaving. They would have probably only said something stupid. I thought it was better just to slip away quietly. I did say goodbye to Iain though.

I thanked him for all his support and told him I wouldn't be trialling next season. He wished me well and said he had something he wanted to show me. He gave me sheet of paper and said I might find it amusing. Earlier in the season Iain had written to a Girls' Centre of Excellence to try and persuade them to send a scout out to watch me play. He'd been unsuccessful, and the sheet was a copy of the reply he received from the lady he'd written to.

Dear Iain,

I am aware of the rules which prevent girls playing for boys' teams beyond U14s. I can assure you that this rule is not changing. I do not necessarily agree with you that Niamh's experience will prove beneficial: the boys' game relies on pace and physicality; the girls (certainly at our GCOE level) places a high priority on the technical aspects as this is what is required for players to cut it in the Women's Super League in this country – the women's game relies a lot more on ability on the ball...

Kind regards,
[Name witheld]

I guess it's one view, but it's not one I share. It's pretty much in line with what the FA brochures were saying about CoEs being the only way into top-level women's football. But it also showed how negativity towards mixed football comes from both sides: men and women. I wondered how much boys' football the person writing the email had actually seen. Not very much I was guessing. It was very hard to imagine being able to play in the A League without technical ability on the ball.

Two days later there was some good news from the FA. They had extended the age limit for playing mixed football again and I was going to be allowed to continue playing with boys at under 15. I was relieved and happy. All I needed to do now was find another club.

Chapter 13
Changing Sides

"It [playing mixed football] wasn't liked. The parents of the opposing teams were a bit jealous because I was a girl and I was better than all their sons. They refused to field a team on two occasions."

Kelly Smith, England women's record goalscorer

For the season ahead the challenge would be to find a team that could give me exactly what I was looking for: a boys' team that had good training (preferably twice a week), played at a decent standard, with the opportunity to get a lot of minutes on the pitch. This time I was much more confident about my own abilities and was looking for a team in either the A or B League. I decided to try out for two of the biggest clubs in the league: Sheffield Wednesday Young Owls and Dronfield Town.

Young Owls, Sheffield Wednesday's community team and one of the top sides, were initially my first choice. They had finished runners-up in the A League and getting into their squad would have felt like a massive achievement for me. Dronfield competed in the B League. They had finished mid-table, but trained twice a week and had the best facilities in the entire league. Their ground was used as the venue for the County Cup finals and was also the home of Sheffield Wednesday's EPDC. Both clubs had great reputations.

First up was Dronfield. Steve, the manager, was expecting me, but he had no idea that I was a girl. We arrived on time,

but most of the lads had got there early and about 15 or
so were having a kickabout. They were all wearing identical
black training kit, except for one lad who I assumed was
another trialist.

As we walked towards the three coaches a now familiar
scenario began to unfold. The one that was obviously Steve
had an increasingly puzzled look on his face.

"Hi, are you Steve?" said Dad. "This is my daughter,
Niamh. I sent you an email about her. She's come for a trial."

Steve nodded and smiled. He looked friendly, but also very
confused.

"Right... you do know this isn't a girls' team, don't you? I
haven't dropped a clanger, have I?"

Dad told him that there was no mistake, but Steve seemed
unsure.

"Are girls actually allowed to play? I didn't think they
could."

There was a lady standing next to him and she confirmed
that the club received a letter from the FA saying that girls
could play up until under 15s. Steve obviously thought that
she knew what she was talking about, but he still looked a
bit shocked.

"But I've never coached a girl before," he said.

"Don't think of her as a girl – just think of her as a
defender," said Dad.

Steve was finally convinced.

"Fair enough. Get yourself warmed up Niamh and we'll
have a look at you."

I walked over to the lads. As usual I could see that they
were laughing, but it was obviously not nasty – again more
down to surprise than anything else. I gave a good account
of myself in the drills, so when we moved on to the practice
match, people were calling my name and I saw a lot of the
ball.

At the end Steve was positive.

"I'll admit, that was a real eye-opener for me," he said. "You can obviously play. And I can see you're not afraid to get stuck in, but I also think there's a few things we can help you to develop and improve on if you come to us."

He asked me to come back the next week, which was a relief in two ways. I had really enjoyed it, but I still had the Young Owls trial coming up so I didn't want to make a decision right away. I said I'd definitely be back the following week.

The Young Owls trials were scheduled to take place over consecutive days. Their manager, Frank, phoned up my dad after he received the email and they had a long discussion, so fortunately he already knew I was a girl. Frank said he was very happy to judge me purely on football ability, but having finished runners-up last season, he was hoping to go one better and win the league this year. In other words, he was looking to strengthen what was already an excellent team.

When we arrived at Sheffield Wednesday's training ground, we were stopped at the entrance by a man in a peaked cap holding a clipboard.

"Can I help you at all?" he asked.

"We've come for the under 15s trials. I think they start at 11am," said Dad.

The man looked at his clipboard for a fraction of a second.

"I'm sorry mate but there's no girls' or ladies' trials taking place here today. They're all up at Chaucer School. You want to get yourselves up there instead."

"Thanks, but no we don't. She's come to try out for the boys' team."

The clipboard man looked horrified and started shaking his head.

"No, no, no. I'm sorry, but that's not allowed. They're not allowed to play together. Boys and girls – it's just not allowed. Now if you hurry, you might make the girls' trial at Chaucer. It's only a mile or so up the road. Sorry love, it's FA rules not ours. It's just not allowed."

"The good news is that you are right: it wasn't allowed in the past, but it is now. That rule was changed only last week," said Dad. "I think if you check your clipboard again, you'll see she's on there. Frank knows she's coming. McKevitt's the name."

Open-mouthed, the clipboard man looked down again, but more thoroughly this time.

"I've got a Knee-ammer Mac-Key-vitt?"

"That'll be her."

The man shook his head, as if to say, 'What is the world coming to? First they give them the vote and now this,' but he knew he had to wave us through.

"Well, you'd best go in then. Pitch One."

The trials for the younger age groups were still taking place, so the under 15 trialists and their parents were all waiting around the entrance to the pitches. I could see that they were looking over at me and, as usual, they were laughing. This time though, it definitely looked like it was in a nasty way. A few were staring and, by the way some of them were laughing, the jokes they were making were probably not the kind you get on children's TV. Clearly one or two thought they were intimidating me. But instead, it just made me even keener to get started.

I was prepared for it. Dad had asked me on the way to the trial how I'd cope if I didn't get on with the lads in the team.

"There'll be a lot of 'Big Time Charlies' at Young Owls," he said. "At least a few will believe they've got a real chance of playing professionally – whether they have or not is another matter. Just don't expect this to be the friendliest club in the world. That's all I'm saying."

"I'm only playing football with them, Dad," I replied. "I'm not looking to be friends with them."

Judging by the first impression of my prospective team-mates, it was a good job I wasn't.

Frank turned up and shook my hand. He was a serious

coach – unusually he didn't have a son in the team – but he seemed friendly enough. The trial started with a few words from Frank about what was going to happen. It was very formal, much more like a CoE training session. Nobody was speaking at all, let alone mucking about. The first thing I noticed was how much bigger the players were. Even at Millhouses I was one of the taller ones, but five or six towered over me at this trial and a few were at least 6ft tall. They looked like an under 18 team.

Frank took no part in the session and left everything to his assistant coaches. He watched us from the touchline. The standard was incredible. Everybody had a great first touch and they all used tricks to make a little bit of space for themselves on the pitch. I was quite happy with the way I'd played. I'd linked up really well with the right-midfielder and was getting up and down the pitch, overlapping and winning most of my headers. I didn't want to be overconfident, but if I didn't get a callback then at least I'd have known I'd done my best. At the end of the match, Frank said that he'd been impressed by everyone, but read out the names of the 18 players that he wanted to come again the following evening. When he called out my name, I tried to look cool as if I wasn't bothered, but inside I was really excited and wanted to punch the air. But the celebrating had to wait until we were back in the car.

On the way home Dad said he thought I'd done really well and given a good account of myself, but warned me not to get carried away.

"I know it would be a real achievement if you get offered a place in this squad, but once that novelty has worn off, you've got the reality of the season to think about. Watching that game impartially I'd say you looked like a good player, but the lad playing right-back on the other team was exceptional. Realistically, if you do get offered a place I think you'll be the back-up option. Maybe you're fine with that, but you've got to bear it in mind when you make your decision. If you went to Dronfield instead, I think you'd get a lot more pitch time."

He'd given me a lot to think about.

The following day we reconvened. Frank said he only wanted to sign 14 players and would let us know who was in and who was out at the end of the night's session. Tonight, I wasn't as pleased with my own performance. I knew I could have done better: not terrible but not great either. I just hadn't played well enough.

Frank sat us down in a circle.

"Now I'm going to go round one by one and let you know whether or not I'm going to offer to sign you. I want you to look me in the eye and let me know for definite whether or not you're going to sign. If you're not then fair enough, but there are others here who need to know whether or not they've a place in the squad."

This really surprised me. I'd be delighted to get a place in this team and couldn't imagine why anyone would have wanted to miss out. But as Frank went round the group and asked, "Are you coming?" the reasons become clear.

"I don't know – depends on how my trial at Rotherham goes."

"I might, but I've got a callback at Sheffield United."

"I can't say yet. I'm waiting to hear back from Chesterfield."

"I'm not sure. I've been asked to trial at Wednesday's academy."

And so it went on.

In the end, six of the lads were waiting to hear whether they'd got places in professional academies before deciding whether they were going to come join this team (including, I am happy to say, the right-back my Dad thought was better than me).

When it came to my turn, Frank said he was impressed – "You were outstanding Niamh" – but that he wasn't going to sign me. I didn't think I was outstanding, so it wasn't a surprise. But while my pride was hurt, what I felt most of all – weirdly – was relief. I would have signed for Young Owls if they'd offered me a place, but I don't think it would have been a good decision. I'm fairly certain that I'd have been warming the bench more often than not.

I wasn't too disappointed and the next evening Dronfield offered me a place in their squad. I was very happy to sign for them. My new team-mates seemed to be a decent bunch and I thought I'd enjoy it there. Steve the coach was really pleased when I told him. He said that they had a good squad of players for the upcoming season, and he also told me that there was some exciting news: at Easter, we were going to Holland to play in an international tournament.

Chapter 14
Playing with the Girls

"To watch people push themselves further than they think they can, it's a beautiful thing. It's really human."

Abby Wambach, US footballer, capped over 240 times and scorer of over 180 international goals

I was now in Year 10 and with only two years left at school I was looking more seriously into the possibility of applying for a college scholarship in the US. The son of one of Mum's colleagues had been offered a golfing scholarship at the University of Minnesota, so she gave us a load of information about the process – what the colleges were looking for, how to apply etc – and provided some useful contacts.

Unsurprisingly, there was no mention of what to do if you were playing mixed football. Dad said that my experience would all pay off once I got to trials, but the trick was getting invited to the trials. He said that university admission departments usually liked applications that are straightforward: they're not geared up to deal with candidates who have unusual backgrounds.

"But, of course, if you do get into the County squad we won't have to worry about it."

After the disappointment of the previous year, I'd been counting down the days until the next trial. I did know one girl from Rovers who had got in the previous season. Libby was a great player and from what she said it sounded brilliant: travelling round the country, playing matches –

a bit like being in a national team. Libby was a year older than me, but she would be trialling again this season. I had no doubt that she'd get in again and I really hoped that I would be joining her.

I knew that the trials would take place towards the end of September. As time moved on I kept expecting to hear something from my school. I asked Miss Nicholls, the head of P.E, a few times, but she said she'd heard nothing. After yet another week without any news, I asked Dad if he had any ideas about what to do.

"I'll get in touch with the coach at the County directly," he said. "Pete emailed me a couple of times following last years mix-up and seemed like a good guy. I'm sure he'll tell us what's happening."

I headed off to school a bit more hopeful that we'd hear something. At home time I turned my phone on and there was a text message from Dad: 'Niamh, County trials are TODAY at 4:30. I've finished work early and have got your kit in the car. Will meet you outside school at 3:30. Dad'

I got outside the gate and, sure enough, there was Dad's car parked across the road.

"How did you find out they were on tonight?" I asked.

"I emailed Pete, the head coach, this afternoon. Two minutes later, he rang me to say they started tonight. He was a bit alarmed you'd not got the message. Apparently he sent an email to Mr O'Sullivan earlier this month with all the details and even said he wanted you to attend. I don't know why you didn't get the message. At least you're going now so no harm done."

It was on the Monday morning following the trial, during P.E, that I got the news. Miss Nicholls addressed the whole class and said, "Now I'm afraid I'm going to embarrass Niamh. I've just been informed that she's been selected to play football for the County. That is a real achievement so I think we should give her a round of applause."

I was delighted, but then everybody started clapping so I did get very embarrassed as well.

I was so excited about making the squad, but it was only on the way home that it hit me. I could have missed out altogether. Not just on playing for the County, but on getting a scholarship as well. If Dad hadn't contacted Pete when he did I would have missed the trial.

My school made a big deal about my selection for the County. First of all they put the story on the front page of the school newsletter and website. Then at the open evenings for new students, they talked up the school's athletic record by saying they had a Year 10 pupil playing football for the County. Parents of my school-friends kept coming up to congratulate me. I thought it was very nice of them to do that, but I was a bit annoyed that the school seemed to be trying to take the credit. They were making it look like they'd helped me to get into the team when in fact, if it had been down to them, I wouldn't even have known about the trial. I talked to Mum and Dad and they said they felt it was 'a bit rich' too.

At parents evening my Head of Year, Mr Lacey, told Dad that the school was "very proud of Niamh's sporting achievement". Dad said that while that was kind of him to say that, I was actually playing for the County despite the school rather than because of it.

Not long after the County trial, I received some more good news. Doncaster Rovers Belles, the Women's Super League team, wrote to me. They had got my address from Derby and wanted to invite me to attend some training sessions with the first-team manager, John Buckley. From not playing with girls at all I was suddenly playing twice a week.

Dronfield Town Boys were having a tough season, but I was very happy with my own performances. Our first two matches were away to teams relegated from the A League.

On paper these were going to be our hardest fixtures. The kick-off for our first game against Ecclesall Rangers was actually delayed slightly because the referee didn't believe I was eligible to play. There were a few minutes of confusion before someone had the bright idea of using their phone to look up the rule change. The ref seemed satisfied by that, if not entirely convinced that it was the best idea he'd ever heard. We led twice in the game, but conceded two goals in the last two minutes and got beaten 4-2. Steve said he could give 'Player of the Match' to either of the centre-backs, but awarded it to Charlie rather than me because he'd moved up two divisions and was playing at this level for the first time.

Our second match was against Rawmarsh, a team I'd played a few times before. I usually had a good game against them. As I walked onto the pitch I overhead one of the Rawmarsh parents say, "Look they've got a girl playing for them. I wonder if she's as good as the girl who plays for Millhouses?"

"She is the girl who played for Millhouses," replied one of our supporters.

I liked hearing that. Those sort of comments gave me confidence. I felt I played another decent game, although we ended up losing. Steve gave me another honourable mention in dispatches.

With what looked like our two most difficult games of the season out of the way, we faced Greasborough, a team promoted from the C League. This was where we thought our season would really begin to take off. In fact, it's where it all began to go wrong. For this match Steve changed the formation. Instead of playing three in the defence and wing-backs he went to a back four. I was okay with that as it meant I was playing in my best position, right-back, but most of the others were used to playing with a back three rather than a back four.

Straight from the kick-off you could tell what kind of game

we were in for. There was a lot of niggly fouls, mouthing-off and little digs off the ball. Some of the lads in our team didn't like that. There was a Greasborough player up against one of our midfielders – who I'll call Dave. He kept telling Dave how crap he was and what was going to happen next time he got the ball. I shouted at Dave to ignore him; that the guy was just being a dick and to try and focus on the game instead, but I could tell it was getting to him. Dave stopped looking for the ball and never seemed to be in a position to receive a pass. He looked to me like he didn't want to be on the pitch. The opposing midfielder kept shouting things to his team-mates like, "Pass it down this side! He's s***!"

I wasn't spared the sledging either. The spanner I was marking clearly thought it was hilarious that he was playing against a girl. He kept laughing directly at me and saying things to his mates like, "This isn't fair! How am I supposed to tackle a girl? I don't want to hurt her."

If he was trying to annoy me, it was working. About half an hour into the game a clearance came my way and I had the chance to put in a header. Spanner wasn't expecting me to make a challenge for it, so I went over the top of him, won the ball and made sure I landed on him as hard as I could. He was outraged, but the referee waved play on. I offered to help him up and said, "This might be your first season in this league mate, but it isn't mine!"

All this happened in front of the Greasborough home supporters who, amazingly, gave me a round of applause. That really spurred me on and made me even more determined that he wouldn't get past me. He didn't. And every time I tackled him his own team's parents clapped and cheered. It was fantastic. Elsewhere on the pitch though, things were not going so well. Greasborough were the worst team we'd played so far, but they went in 2-0 up at half time and put another four past us in what was becoming a typical late second-half collapse.

Steve was furious during the team talk at the end of the game. He said it was a spineless performance: we'd been battered by a side no better than us because too many players had been hiding on the pitch and we should be ashamed of ourselves. I agreed with everything he said. He paused just before the end.

"Right, Player of the Match? Easy this week – Niamh! The only one out of the lot of you who wasn't afraid to put a challenge in. Perhaps the rest of you should start playing like girls. See you all at training on Tuesday!"

On the way off the pitch a few of the Greasborough parents came over to tell me they thought I'd played well. The spanner came over too. I thought, 'Oh no, he's going to have another go at me.' But instead he put out his arm to shake hands.

"Well played, mate. You had a right game today. You're the only reason we didn't score 10!"

"Thanks. You were the better team." I said.

I like this part of football. I don't mind the sledging on the pitch and the mind games – in fact I think it's a better game because of it – but at the end of the match it should all stay on the pitch. I left thinking, 'He's a decent guy.' He'd been trying to wind me up and it hadn't worked, but his team had still won. Fair play to him.

Incidents like this make me think that people should consider the bigger picture where mixed football is concerned. In my opinion, a lot of unnecessary health and safety research has been done, but hardly any into the attitudes of the boys who play with and against girls. I'd been playing in the top leagues for four seasons. I'm not one of the best players, but I do stand out. Yet the sniggering usually only ever happens the first time I've played against a team. The second time we play, they just think of me as an opposition player. With my own team-mates, the process of acceptance is even quicker. All that matters is, can you play? Are you a player? Will you help us win? Whether you're a boy or a girl is completely unimportant.

For good reasons, my teams' supporters will also tell you that the novelty of watching me play wears off really quickly. Sure it's interesting at first, but I'm a defender, not Lionel Messi. When did you go to a game in the hope that you'd be watching your team defend? Within 15 minutes they're usually just thinking of me as one of the players. And this is all I am. I have good games and bad games like everyone else. But I love football and I just want to be the best player I can be.

We'd lost three on the spin and just been battered 6-0, but I really did feel that personally I'd never been playing better. After training on Tuesday Steve said that the FA had been in touch. They were conducting some research into mixed football and had asked if I would be willing to participate. I was very happy to be involved and he gave Dad the contact details of Rachel Pavlou, the FA's National Development Manager for Women's Football. A few days later Dr Laura Hills, an expert in youth sport from Brunel University who was leading the research, contacted us.

Dear Steve and Niamh,

Thank you for agreeing to take part. We are currently conducting research for the FA on mixed-gender football. We have been working with them since the age limit was under 11 so have seen quite a few changes.

As far as we know, Niamh is the only girl playing at this level. We believe there may be other girls involved but she is the only one we have been able to verify in this age group. We are going to observe Niamh's team over the next few months and submit our report to the FA in January. The observation involves two researchers attending the match and completing an observation schedule.

Best regards
Dr Laura Hills
Senior Lecturer
School of Sport and Education
University of Brunel

I was really happy to be involved, but surprised to find out that I was the only girl in the country playing under 15 mixed football. I knew I was the only girl in the league, but had always imagined that there would be loads of others spread across the country. It felt weird to think that any extension to the rule, that I was so desperate to happen, would be down to what the researchers made of my performances for Dronfield. For the first time I felt like I actually had some influence over the politics.

I was able to carry my form over into the County team. I managed to get a place in the starting 11 for the first match and stayed there for the whole season. It was great to be playing girls' football at such a good standard and it was a lot more fun than playing for Derby. Pete Harper was an excellent coach. At training he tended just to work exclusively on set plays, shape and tactics, rather than fitness or training drills, so it was really enjoyable. I was loving the opportunity to beat players with pace. Knowing I was faster than the winger I was marking gave me much more confidence to get forward.

Again it was very difficult to compare the girls' and boys' games I was playing in at this time. I wouldn't say one was better than the other. The County game was a lot quicker and more physical than grassroots girls' football, but it wasn't as physical or as quick as the boys' game. I can honestly say I don't remember losing a 50/50 while I was playing for the County. Nor did I experience that explosive speed that you find in boy's football. County teams were more likely to try and pass the ball round me than run at me. But there's no doubt in my mind that South Yorkshire Under 16 Girls could have more than held their own in one of the boys' leagues.

Results at Dronfield failed to pick up, but I still felt I was doing well. I was also playing full games for the County and Pete singled me out for praise quite a few times. I was full of confidence and in the best form of my life. On the way home from another painful defeat with Dronfield – despite winning 3-2 with five minutes to go we ended up losing 6-3 – Dad told me he had some very good news.

"Obviously we know there's no chance of playing for England because you're not at a Centre of Excellence, but how would you feel about playing for Ireland instead?"

I said I didn't know what he meant.

"Because Mum's Irish you've got dual citizenship, so you are qualified to play for Ireland. The Republic has always had English-based players in the squad, so I sent your CV to Dave Connell, the under 17 manager.

"Dave got back in touch this morning. He said you are eligible for the under 16 team and wants to take a look at you. He's given their manager, Sharon Boyle, your details and said they're going to invite you over for a trial the next time the squad gets together."

I was speechless. I've always felt a part of me was Irish – it's hard not to when half your family's from over there and you've a name like mine – and I'd always joked about playing for Ireland in the World Cup, but I never believed that it could actually happen.

Chapter 15
Dea-scéal & Goede tidjen

"When I was playing, they said soccer was a man's world and women should remain on the sidelines. All I can say is, I'm glad I never had to go up against Mia Hamm."

Pelé

I didn't have to wait long for the Football Association of Ireland (FAI) to organise things. Two weeks later, at the beginning of December, I was on a plane over to Dublin for yet another trial. I'd been to Ireland quite a few times – almost all of Mum's family live over there – but I wasn't sure what to expect. I didn't know whether I'd be the only English-based girl at the trial or how the other players would react to me. Mum said she thought it would be fine and everyone would be very friendly. Dad agreed. He said there was such a strong tradition of emigration from Ireland that foreign-based players were the norm rather than the exception.

I got to the training ground with plenty of time to spare. The pitches at the national training ground were fantastic, but this was where the difference between football in the UK and Ireland really hit home. Ireland has less than 10 per cent of the population of England and 'soccer' is not the national sport. The Gaelic sports – football and hurling – are much bigger. My granddad played hurling at County level and was a goalkeeper for Carlow. He's football mad now, played a lot when he was young and even managed teams, but he didn't know anything about the game at all until he moved to London when he was 18. He started playing in goal for a Sunday league team, but he didn't understand the rules. The rest of the team were screaming, "Use your area!" but he didn't know what that meant. He said he was quite surprised to discover that he was the only one allowed to pick the ball up.

There is professional men's football but The League of Ireland does not compare with the Football League, let alone the Premier League. There is very little money in the game so all the best players are overseas. The facilities at Dronfield Town were great. We had a huge, brand new clubhouse and 3G pitches for training and winter matches. Pitches aside, the facilities at the national training ground were a bit spartan, but it's what goes on when you're on the pitch that's important and, despite these challenges, Ireland was on the way to becoming one of the best women's teams in Europe. The under 17s were runners up in the UEFA Championship in 2010, while the under 19s reached the semi-finals of their equivalent competition in 2014. I was under no illusions about how hard it was going to be to get a place in the squad.

Mum was right – everyone I met was very friendly. I was in fact the only girl from England, but by now I was used to being the odd one out. Not that odd this time, though. Not only were there four other Niamhs in the squad, but there was even another McKevitt. Right away that made me feel like I fitted in. We had a series of training sessions in the morning and a friendly match in the afternoon. I was wondering how the standard would compare with the various places I'd played. I know it's funny, but before I got there I was half expecting that an international team would look different. Yet, when I arrived and the players were standing around in their tracksuits chatting, they didn't look any different to a decent grassroots or CoE team. They weren't bigger or superhuman looking: they were normal sized. I don't know why that should have surprised me, but it did. I've met several professional footballers, both men and women, and it's always something of a surprise to find they're normal sized or even smaller than me.

Two minutes into the first drill, a high-intensity exercise carried out at a sprint without any mistakes, it was apparent that the standard was much higher than anywhere I'd played before – either girls' or boys' football. That wasn't a surprise though, because this was the 22 best under 16 girls in Ireland. But it wasn't just the ability that was different: it was the attitude. All the players at Ireland wanted to be the best they could be. There were no weak links. There was no one who shouldn't have been there; no one you looked at and thought, 'What are you doing here?' The coaches were looking for excellence, not competence. Every one there was capable; everyone deserved to be at that level, but it was only going to be those who proved themselves to be extraordinary, who gave more than any of the others gave, who would get into the team.

Even playing at County or CoE level in England you come across quite a few girls who either don't really want to go further with football or haven't got the attitude to go as far as they can. There are other people who think that getting into a team is an end rather than a beginning: and others still with talent and ability who don't want to get out of their comfort zone. At Derby and Sheffield United there had been a lot of talk about being elite, but at Ireland it really felt like it was elite. It didn't feel contrived. This wasn't a bunch of players turning up to some amazing training facility and thinking, 'Aren't we brilliant?'

I felt I put in a good performance in the friendly, playing the whole match and winning 2-0. The coaches, Sharon Boyle and Sean Byrne, were really positive after the game.

"You were outstanding Niamh, exactly what we're looking for," said Sharon.

"We get a lot of girls contacting us about coming over to trials, and it's grand to have someone come over who's at the required standard," said Sean.

To hear Sharon and Sean say those things was encouraging. The next get-together was going to be in February. I'd have to wait over two months to find out whether I'd make the squad or not, but I was feeling, if not confident, then at least positive about my chances.

I've got Ireland to thank for reigniting my passion for women's football. I had been dreading having to return to the women's game. I had tried grassroots and Centres of Excellence and much preferred boys' football. The television coverage of the WSL, on the digital sport channel *ESPN*, had also been really disappointing. What I had been hoping for was a version of the established format: a studio with a presenter and a couple of ex-players giving the week's games a bit of analysis; a kind of *Match of the Day for Women's Football* if you like. Instead, *ESPN*'s coverage was patronising. It looked like it was put together by people who knew very little about football and assumed that their audience didn't either. There was some woman I'd never heard of presenting from the side of the pitch, while a hand-held camera zoomed in for wacky angles. She interviewed players who looked less than thrilled to be involved. Player interviews are always terrible – even in the men's game – and these were no exception. We'd discover players who were 'taking each game as it comes', 'pleased with the performance' and 'working hard in training'. In between were a few clips of the actual matches with some rubbish commentary. In other words, almost totally unwatchable. I tried sitting through the show twice and then gave up on it altogether. I didn't know anyone else who'd watched it either. Certainly, *ESPN*'s coverage of the WSL never made me feel like I wanted to be playing there.

I wasn't expecting the FA to extend the mixed football rule to under 16 for the following season and, before the Ireland trial, I had come to the decision that, if they didn't, I'd just give football up and do something else instead. But Ireland had completely changed my mind. Playing there made me feel that there really was an elite women's game and, if I could play in that, then that's where I wanted to be. I felt that with the experience I'd gained I was ready to make the step-up into the adult game.

I talked to Dad about it when I was back in England. He agreed that perhaps a move up to adult, open-age football was probably a good idea, but said that there were some things to consider. I was only 15 and had eighteen months to go at school before my GCSEs next year. Regardless of whether I was good enough or not, how would I find the social challenge of playing with women who could be as much as 20 years older than me? It would be a completely different experience to junior football.

I spoke to Richard Stevenson, who'd done a lot of coaching in the women's game. He gave me quite a bit of good advice and seemed to know a lot about the teams in the area. He was doing some work with a local women's team who played in the County league, but recommended I look "a few divisions higher for a club on the way up.'

I also contacted Duncan Milligan, then the first-team coach at Doncaster Belles. I'd been training with Belles, enjoyed it there and liked Duncan. He invited me for a trial with their development squad, but only in a year's time once I was 16. That felt like too long to wait.

There was some surprising good news, however. The FA researchers said they were recommending a further increase in the age limit. That meant that, if I wanted to, I'd be able to carry on playing with lads for another season. I was very happy to have so many options for once.

I was called up by Ireland for another training camp in February. I thought it went well and I must have done enough because I made the squad for the next international game in

April – against England. I was really excited. To be honest, if I could have picked the opponents for my first game, it would have been England. I was so determined to do well. I couldn't have been more up for it.

As the only UK-based player, I hooked up with the rest of the squad at the team hotel in Derby. We were playing England at St George's Park in Burton. The £105m training ground, purpose-built for 24 England teams, was a far cry from our own facilities. We spent two days training at St George's prior to the match, which was good because it was easy to be overawed by the place.

Being away with the team was great, but it wasn't like a school trip or a holiday. After a day's training, I was too exhausted to do much more than chill out on my bed watching TV or listening to music. Our whole lifestyle was carefully managed. Upon joining the squad I was given a food and exercise diary, which had to be signed off as a true and accurate record by my parents. There was an emphasis on strength and conditioning, which all players were expected to take responsibility for themselves.

What I ate was also carefully monitored. It was fruit and porridge for breakfast and chicken and pasta for everything else. There was no helping myself to the hotel breakfast buffet. At one training camp, a new girl on our table unknowingly filled her plate with a 'Full Irish' breakfast. We warned her to ditch the fry-up quickly and get muesli and fruit like the rest of us before the coaches caught her. The match against England was kicking off at 11am so we were given yet more chicken and pasta for breakfast, which we all thought was a bit strange.

England didn't have an under 16 team so we were up against their under 17s. I got the impression they thought they were going to win easily. Like us, they knew Ireland's under 15s had been well-beaten the day before, but I was confident that we had enough about us to give any side a game. It's true there are a lot fewer people in Ireland, but in a way I think that's an advantage. There is no academy system, so all the girls play in what is effectively a national grassroots league. It's a system that has its benefits. Firstly the standard of play and coaching is much higher than in English grassroots leagues, and secondly, unlike girls in CoEs, the Irish girls are used to playing in a competitive league. There will be sports psychologists who disagree, but I think that the pressure of knowing you need to win a game is one of the most exciting aspects of playing football. Nothing beats the build-up to the big matches that can lead to promotion, relegation, winning the league or the next round of the cup. That desire for success and determination to win is certainly a feeling that I missed when I was playing at a CoE.

I started on the bench, but at half time, with the match 0-0, I was given my chance. It was an amazing feeling running onto the pitch in my international kit, but I didn't really have time to soak it up and enjoy it at the time. International football is a very technical game and my head was full of the instructions Sean had given me before I came on.

I was playing right-midfield. We were to let England have the ball when they were in their third, but press them immediately when they came into the middle third of the pitch. My job was to cut out the diagonal passes the left-back was making into the middle of the park and force her to play it down the outside. It was a lot harder than it sounds but I managed it.

It was a tough game, played at an incredible pace, but we were far happier with the result than England. A 0-0 draw, away from home against allegedly higher-ranked opposition is a great achievement in international football. I was exhausted, but the atmosphere in the dressing room was fantastic. Sean and Sharon were delighted with the performance, which felt like the culmination of a lot of hard work. Not that there was much time to enjoy it. Half an hour after the game I was in the car on my way home as the rest of the squad flew back to Dublin. It had been a great experience but before long I was back to wondering whether or not I'd be included in the squad for the next match.

The England game had given me my first taste of international football, but I wasn't going to have to wait long for my second. Ten days later, at 2:30am on Good Friday morning, I was getting on a coach to Manchester Airport as Dronfield Town headed into Europe to play in the Stormvogels Easter Tournament in Amsterdam.

This time Dad came with me. At the start of the season there had been a meeting about the trip. Dronfield sent an under 15 team over to Holland every year and there was a lot of fundraising required to pay for it. The club had also asked for parent volunteers to go along with the team. My dad put his hand up immediately. He said there was no way he'd be able to stay at home while his daughter went to Holland on her own with a bunch of 15-year-old lads.

"Niamh's mum would kill me!" he said.

I was looking forward to Amsterdam but I was wondering how we'd all get on. As committed to mixed football as I am, and while I believe there is no difference in football ability, I can confirm that teenage boys and girls are nothing like each other socially. Over the past three years, I'd noticed quite a few interesting things about how teenage boys behave when they're together. If there were times when it had felt that mixed football was giving me a unique insight into the male psyche, then the Amsterdam tournament could have been a research project.

By now I'd known most of the team for the best part of a year. I got on with some lads better than others, but they were a decent bunch on the whole. I knew they thought I was a good player. I usually got the ball when I called for it and there would be enthusiastic praise if I won the ball during a match. They'd also let me know if they thought I was playing badly and tell me to "eff-off" if I went in too hard in training. I didn't mind at all because it just meant I was being treated as one of the lads.

However, it's very easy to get treated as one of the lads if you look like one of the lads. As I turned up for the bus it dawned on me that they'd only ever seen me in football kit with my hair tied up and we were all in normal clothes for this trip. As was usual when I wasn't playing football, which was most of the time, I was wearing normal clothes, make-up and had my hair down. It was as if, for the first time ever, the lads had noticed that I was actually a girl. It's not that anyone fancied me or anything like that – and I'm sure none of them did – but if you've ever seen how 15-year-old boys behave when they're around girls, you'll know that they tend not to treat them as one of the lads. At the very least it's an opportunity for them to show off and take the piss out of each other.

I sat on my own on the coach, but I was quite happy about it because I didn't really want anyone next to me. But even the boys I got on well with were too scared to join me. Jack, a lad I'd known for years because, like me, he'd joined Dronfield from Millhouses, came over to ask if he could borrow my phone charger. I gave it to him and he headed back to his own seat. As he did, all the lads on the back seat – the alpha males – started taking the mickey.

"Hey look at Hibbo everyone! He's trying to get in with Niamh and she's booted him right into the 'team-mate zone'. Not even the 'friend zone', the 'team-mate zone'. 'Sorry, Jack we're just team-mates'. Hibbo's in the 'team-mate zone!'"

Poor Jack – that was the last time he spoke to me all trip. He even sent his little brother over to return my charger.

We were staying at Center Parcs just outside Amsterdam and we were all allocated chalets. Quite a few other parents had come so I was sharing with Dad and some of the other parents. I was secretly quite pleased that none of the other lads were in with us. We arrived at about 9am on Good Friday. The tournament didn't start until the following day and finished on Sunday evening, so that gave us a whole day in Center Parcs to do whatever we wanted. The dads pretty much all headed for the bar. Dad gave me 40 euros, told me not to leave the complex and keep my mobile on, but otherwise to go and have fun.

There was lots of stuff to do at Center Parcs including a massive indoor swimming pool, loads of outdoor activities and cycling. After dumping my stuff, I met up with the rest of the team and we talked about what we were going to do. There were a few suggestions, but three of the lads had managed to get hold of two crates of lager, so when it was put to a vote we all decided to go back to their chalet and drink them. I got the impression that preparation for this tournament was not going to have the same high standards as I'd experienced with Ireland.

There was an air of inevitability about what happened next. Most people had a few bottles of lager: a few people had most of the bottles of lager. It was a really good laugh – for most people. For 'The Few' it was something they later all swore they'd 'never do again'. Somebody said that drinking on an empty stomach was asking for trouble, so we all headed off to the restaurant and ordered pizza and chips ('What would Sean or Sharon have thought,' I wondered).

After lunch, the sober ones among us went swimming. I came out of the changing room and saw all the lads were standing in the queue for the biggest water slide. The swimming area was full of other kids, including several pretty Dutch girls. Three of them were sitting in the jacuzzi. I joined them and they smiled at me and said "Hello".

"Where are you from?" asked a slim girl with blonde hair.

"I'm from Sheffield in England. And you?" I said

"We three are from Maastricht. This is Famke and Anouk. Their English is very little. My name is Fay."

"Hi, I'm Niamh."

"Hi," said Anouk and Famke.

Fay could speak a little English. I learned that the girls were a couple of years younger than me and that they were school friends on a family holiday.

"Your family is here also?" asked Fay.

I tried to explain that I was there for a football tournament.

"Ah football! Yes I know this – where is your team?"

I pointed in the direction of the wave pool where Fez and Brad were trying to pull off James' shorts, and our midfielders were having a competition to see who could hold their breath underwater the longest.

"Most of them are over there," I said.

After my extended exposure to the lads it was a nice break to be chatting with girls. Outside football I'd never spent so much time with my team-mates before. Without a ball to occupy them they seemed to spend 75 per cent of the time taking the piss out of each other. The slightest mispronunciation was seized upon and a double meaning was wrung out of every sentence.

"Does anyone want to play..." Sam might say.

Shot down before he could finish, fingers pointed in accusation,

"Ahhh 'Play!' Cuttsy said 'Play' everyone! Did you hear him? Yeah we all know what he wants to play with..."

That sort of thing. Repeated forever. Boys must have to be on their guard all the time.

What little conversation they had revolved exclusively around three subjects:

The Premier League: I liked watching it, but didn't really follow a team.

FIFA 14: I'll have a go on the PlayStation now and again,

but I have very little to say about this either.

Girls: girls they fancy/what they'd like to do with girls they fancy/what they claim to have done with girls they fancy. I have nothing to contribute at all on this subject.

The rest of the time – and this really was a surprise – they spent singing. They were always bursting into song. On the coach to the tournament there had been variations on what the 'Dronny Boys' were going to do with the local beer and women, but their repertoire had gradually extended to the favourite terrace anthems of Sheffield United and Sheffield Wednesday.

They'd start singing in the security queue at the airport, on the way to the restaurant, when we were waiting for the coach and even on one memorable occasion (although obviously, I only heard this) when they all went to the toilets at the same time.

Singing. All the time. Day and night. Whenever there was a 10-second lull in the Premier League/*FIFA 14*/Girls dialogue one of them would start and the rest always joined in. It was like being trapped in the worst ever episode of *High School Musical*.

So I was enjoying this opportunity to make small talk, which felt quite highbrow in comparison.

I don't know who it was that spotted me first, but suddenly the final of the underwater breathing competition lost its life or death significance and Anouk, Famke, Fay and I were joined in the jacuzzi by a good two-thirds of the Dronfield Town Under 15 Boys football squad. They crammed together on the opposite side of the jacuzzi, smiling broadly in what they thought was a cool and friendly manner. I just thought, 'Oh for God's sake!' but I imagined the Dutch girls found it a bit unnerving.

"Hey Niamh, can you introduce us to your friends?" said Joe.

"These are them," I said.

"Oh Hello," said Fay.

"Hello," said Dronfield Town Under 15 Boys.

"Ask them what their names are, Niamh," said Nick.

"You know, you could ask them yourself." I said.

"But I don't know how to speak German," said Nick.

"Neither do I. And anyway they're Dutch, so they probably don't speak German either."

"What language do they speak?" asked Joe.

"Dutch," I sighed.

"Do you speak Dutch then?" said Nick.

"No I don't, but they also speak English. At least Fay does."

"Ask them where they're from," said Joe.

"Geez! Are you actually listening? Why don't you ask them where they're from, Joe? In English. I just told you Fay can understand English. There isn't some secret language exclusive to girls that you don't know about."

I was now beginning to doubt some of the stories about how successful my team was with the girls of Dronfield. Joe decided to make conversation.

"Alright?" he said, offering out to his hand for them to shake.

As opening lines go it's not the smoothest I've ever heard, but the rest of the team clearly thought that Joe was on to something.

"Alright?" said Nick, offering his hand in exactly the same way as Joe.

Within a few seconds there were six or seven Dronfield Town Under 15 Boys' hands waiting to be shook, each accompanied by an, "Alright?"

The Dutch girls looked baffled. There was a brief discussion – in Dutch – before Fay turned to me and asked, "How do you make them... erm... stop?"

"I not sure that you can," I said. "I think they're like this all the time. You should really be thankful that they're not singing."

"Do any of you girls like football?" asked Jake.

As one, the Dutch girls got out of the jacuzzi and headed towards the lockers.

"Ahh, Jake just got mugged off! The German girls friend zoned Jake!" shouted Joe.

This was accompanied by a great deal of finger pointing before they all started splashing water at him. Then there was a brief pause. I knew what was coming. Sure enough Lewis started singing about 'Dronny Boys' and all the others joined in. The 'German girls' were instantly forgotten, but I decided to follow their example and left the boys to their sing-along (which was cut short when one of the lifeguards came over and told them all to be quiet).

I met up with the Dutch girls again in the changing rooms. They were with a couple of slightly older friends.

"You are with those boys?" asked Fay.

"Yes, they're in the football team I play for. We're playing in a tournament tomorrow."

"Only you?"

"Yes, I'm the only girl in the team."

"Only girl? With them?!"

I nodded. Fay and Anouk scrunched their faces into pitying frowns.

"We feel…"

Fay couldn't think of the English word and said something to the older girls in Dutch, who nodded.

"She says, 'We feel very sorry for you'," said the older girl.

"Yes!" said Fay. "Very sorry for you."

She put a consoling arm on my shoulder and Anouk gave me a friendly hug.

"We are here all weekend if you need us," said Fay.

After the swim, I met up with the lads in the main reception area. Cuttsy had noticed that there was a five-a-side pitch and so six of us decided to get a ball and have a kickabout. There were a few Dutch lads playing already so we challenged them to a match. They seemed to find it very funny that a team with a girl was asking them for a game, but they were friendly enough. Overly friendly perhaps.

"Can the beautiful girl play on our side?" one of them asked.

My team-mates looked as if they had absolutely no idea what he was talking about.

"You are very beautiful," he said, pointing at me.

"What Niamh?" said Cuttsy, sounding genuinely amazed.

"No, we need her in defence. Here you can have Nick. He's s***!"

Nick stopped smiling as Joe pushed him towards the Dutch lads. They weren't being fobbed off that easily.

"We would much rather have the beautiful girl."

"Erm, no, no, you're okay," I said blushing with embarrassment, suddenly feeling very much like the Dutch girls in the pool must have felt. "You can have Nick. He really is s***!"

The rest of Dronfield Town Under 15 Boys thought that was absolutely hilarious.

When it was dinner time, I went to find Dad. He was in the bar where I'd left him at lunchtime with the other parents. There were a lot of empty glasses on the table.

"Hi Dad, you having a good time?"

"I'm having the best Good Friday ever!" he said slowly, pointing at the table full of empty glasses. "How has your day been?"

"Pretty good," I said, "although if this has been a plan to put me off boys for life you'll be pleased to know it's worked!"

All the parents started laughing, and some of the mums invited me to join them for dinner. I didn't need to be asked twice.

The following day we travelled by coach to the Stormvogels tournament. There were teams from all over Europe playing. The facilities were amazing. As I said, Dronfield had a good set up, but this was something else. Stormvogels is really just a grassroots club, but it put Sheffield Wednesday's training ground to shame.

We entered through the clubhouse, which had a nice bar and cafe. Behind that was the main pitch, a 3,000 capacity stadium, and beyond that were four full-sized grass pitches and two 4G pitches, all surrounded by barriers to keep spectators from encroaching. I didn't know if this was standard for Dutch clubs – Dad seemed to think that it was – but I'd never seen anything like it before. There were much closer links between grassroots and professional teams in Holland; the whole of football is much more integrated. So despite the fact that the top Dutch league, the Eredivisie, is nothing like as wealthy as the Premier League, there is much more money in the grassroots game than there is in England. No wonder Holland produce so many good players.

The first day of the tournament was set aside for the group matches. There were 12 teams in two groups of six. Games were 11-a-side, 25 minutes long with no half time. Today we had five matches. In our group were two Dutch teams – including the hosts – a team from Italy and a side from Turkey.

Dronfield's biggest problem all season had been scoring goals. The team actually had more than enough good defenders, but because there were weaker players in other areas, a lot of these tended to get played out of position. We had no attackers at all. In fact, the best strikers in the team were Jack and James, who were both defenders. The only other guy who could play up front, Zach, was our best midfielder. During the season Steve had tried to spread our good players throughout the team, but that just created holes and we conceded too easily. Nobody was expecting this tournament to be any different. However, while the top three in each group went into 'The Stormvogels Cup' the following day, the bottom three went into a 'Stormvogels Plate', so we were definitely guaranteed two days of football.

After a disappointing season confidence in the camp wasn't very high.

"I'm liking the sound of the Plate," said Joe. "That's just our kind of thing: a cup for losers. We've proven how good we are at that consistently over the whole season."

"Yeah," said Jack, "look on the bright side. There might actually be a team here that is worse than us. We might not lose every game."

"And what other team here has an international player?" said Zach pointing at me.

"Just don't tell anyone it's the girl," said Cuttsy.

Steve read the teamsheet out. He'd made a few changes and seemed to be taking the tournament quite seriously. We were going to be playing four at the back: Harry, Jack, Lewis and me. My enthusiasm rose. This was the best back four in my opinion, although Steve had never played us all together before.

Our first match was on the main pitch in front of the big stand against the team from Turkey. The stand was full of the players from other teams in the tournament. Surprise, surprise, they laughed when I came out onto the pitch. During our game they started cheering ironically whenever I got the on the ball. Clearly sexism is not just an English thing.

It wasn't long into the tournament before a few things became apparent. Firstly, none of the other teams played like us. The Turkish side were typical. They tried to keep possession with lots of slow, sideways passes building up through the midfield before trying to play balls quickly into the strikers who made runs between the full-backs and centre-backs.

They were really skilful players with lots of tricks. Like a lot of English teams we were much more direct, trying to get the ball forwards as quickly as possible, so we conceded possession a lot more. On the other hand, they were nowhere near as physical as we were. There were niggly fouls off the ball: grabbing, scratching and shirt pulling, and lots of what we call 'afters' – leaving studs in or kicks after the ball had gone and the ref wasn't looking, that sort of thing – but they really didn't like being tackled at all. As soon as you touched them they went down. And usually rolled around on the ground demanding a free kick.

I noticed the left-winger had this trick where he pretended to take a shot and as players turned to make the block he feinted and pushed the ball past them. He did it every time. When he next came towards me I set myself up knowing that he'd run at me rather than pass it. Sure enough he made the feint, so I hit him as hard as I could. I went in for the challenge, put the ball out for a throw, and clattered into him. He started rolling round on the floor with one arm over his face crying as if he'd broken his leg. The ref indicated a throw-in but he still stayed down. I put my hand out to pull him up so we could get on with the game, but he slapped it away.

"For God's sake," I shouted at him. "Get up you pussy!"

I was right in front of the spectators. I had assumed that none of them would be able to speak English. Wrong. The Dutch team standing behind the barrier all looked shocked for a second by what they'd heard, went silent for a moment but then burst out laughing. They pointed at the kid on the floor and started shouting "pussy" at him. He jumped up immediately, miraculously recovered, and started yelling back at them. The ref had to come over and intervene.

Although we didn't manage a shot at goal, the defence played really well and Joe, Tyler, Zach and Cuttsy worked hard in midfield so we came out with a 0-0 draw. That felt pretty good to be honest. Our first point since Christmas!

It's important not to lose your first game in a tournament.

And in fact we didn't lose a game on the first day and – beyond our wildest dreams – actually qualified for the winners' tournament. We only scored one goal, and no one was more surprised by that than Jamie who put the ball in the net, but at least we could go home having achieved something.

It did make me think that if we'd just concentrated on getting the defence right we wouldn't have done much better during the season, but that was in the past now. English football often gets slagged off but we'd held our own in the tournament and qualified. We lost two games the following day but drew the rest to finish a creditable fifth out of 12 overall.

It was easy to forget that we might have struggled in our league, but there were still six divisions below us. Dronfield wasn't the best team ever, but it was a long way from being the worst. The good performance in the tournament was a great way to finish my time there.

Chapter 16
The Long Goodbye

"The FA's decision is brilliant. If we want to make women's football the best it can possibly be, that's the route we have to go down. At Manchester City we have the chance to train with the under 18 boys and we really enjoy that. They're quicker and more physical than us, but in terms of technical ability we can match them."

Steph Houghton, England captain for the 2015 FIFA World Cup, talking about the mixed football extension to under 16s in 2014

The season was over and I'd told Dronfield that I was leaving. Amsterdam had been great, but Steve wasn't looking to shake up the squad, so I thought I'd take my chances somewhere else.

"I think I've found you a potential club," said Dad. "You've got a trial tomorrow night at Huddersfield Town Ladies if you fancy it?"

"Oh, okay," I said.

I was waiting for the decision from the FA yet again. The alternative to mixed football would be going back to girls' football at under 18, which wasn't something I was wildly enthusiastic about. Even at Huddersfield Town, who had a good under 18 side.

"You don't sound very enthusiastic," said Dad.

I felt a bit bad. He'd put loads of effort into finding me clubs over the years.

"No, I am. I'm sure under 18 will be really good, it's just... you know... going back to girls' football. I'd rather stay playing with the boys if I can."

He started laughing.

"It's not girls football Niamh, it's *women's* football. Your trial is with the senior squad at Huddersfield. Since we spoke to Richard, I've been looking around for a team on the up."

At the time, Huddersfield were top of the Northern Combination. If they got three points from their last three games, they'd be promoted to the Premier League. Dad had sent my CV to the club and their manager, Glen Preston, got back in touch and offered me a trial.

Suddenly I was very enthusiastic. And even more so when Dad showed me Glen's email.

Hi Steve,

I would like to invite Niamh and yourself to come down to training next week to get a base line for the standards of our First XI (which I have to say is very high).

We are a club that considers ourselves to be very modern in our approach. We implement sophisticated tactics that you would expect at professional levels. 90 per cent of the work we do is with a ball, even our fitness training.

The sessions we run will be intense and hard work, but as Niamh has been used to playing with boys that will be of great advantage.

Warmest regards,
Glen

That sounded like something I wanted to be a part of. I especially liked the fact that Glen viewed my mixed-football experience as something positive. Very few others I'd met in the women's game in England had.

There never seems to be an end in football, just the start of something else. I'd never wanted to play for anyone as much as Millhouses... until I tried out County... which lasted until I went to Ireland. Now Huddersfield Town went straight to the top of the wish list.

I could tell right away I was going to like playing for Glen. I liked the way he spoke to me, the way he talked about the game and the way he wanted it to be played. It was a bit disconcerting when the rest of the squad turned up in their own cars, though. But this was a women's team and some of the players were almost twice my age. There were a distinct lack of parents knocking about, so I was glad that Dad had slipped away quietly and left me to it. The rest of the squad were friendly and I was slightly reassured that I appeared to be one of the tallest, but as they chatted about going out and work – and it became clear that a couple of them were teachers – I was worried about how a school kid was going to fit in.

But then I reminded myself that they weren't talking about *FIFA 14* and nobody looked remotely like they were going to burst into song, so I started to feel a bit better about it. The standard was really high but I enjoyed it. At the end Glen asked if I was available the following evening for a friendly against FC United of Manchester, so I thought it must have gone okay.

The match against FC United was much more physical than any girl's game I'd played in previously, but it was all the better for that. The pace was very fast and there was lots more movement off the ball. When we were in possession it was all about giving each other options, and when we didn't have the ball it was about getting in position to win it back. Town played a high-intensity style: lots of possession, short passing through the midfield, no long balls. When they didn't have the ball, they pressed really high up the pitch to win it back (the target when we lost the ball was to win it back within eight seconds).

After the game Dad came over all smiles.

"You're in!" he said. "You'd better talk to Glen."

I couldn't believe it. I was expecting weeks of trials before I found out.

"I've seen enough," said Glen. "You did well and I think you've got a lot of potential. You're a good player, but there are things we need to work on if you're ever going to become an amazing player. If you'd like to join us we'll start you out in the reserves, but if you work hard and listen, I'd hope that you'll be pushing for a place in the first team before too long."

It was such a strange feeling. I knew there was a lot of work to be done, and it wasn't like Glen had said I was a brilliant player or anything, but this was everything I'd been working towards. This was 'it'. I was going to be training twice a week with a Premier League club and hoping to fight my way into the first team. There had to be a catch... and there was.

At my first training session I met David Mallin, the club chairman. He explained that there was a 'slight problem' with my registration. The minimum age for open-age football in England is 16. I could continue to come to training and could even play in friendly matches, but I would have to wait seven months until my birthday in December before I was allowed to play in either the Premier League or the FA Cup. Glen told me not to worry. Just to keep coming to training, working hard and that he would play me in as many friendlies as possible.

"I know seven months seems like a long time, but you'll be 16 before you know it. Once you're 16 there will be a lot of opportunities for you here."

I was really disappointed at first – It doesn't matter how many setbacks you have, you never get used to them – but that feeling didn't last long though. Dad tried to reassure me.

"I don't think it's such bad news. First of all, there's definitely a place for you here, which is great, so that means that for the next seven months you can just enjoy your football without having to worry about the future. That's the first time that's happened in a long while."

So that's what I did.

A few weeks later there was a bonus. I had a phone call from Rachel Pavlou at the FA.

"We won't be announcing this officially until after the weekend so please treat this as confidential, but I thought you'd like to know and I wanted to tell you myself. I've just come from the FA Annual Shareholders' Meeting. We presented the report from Laura Hills' team at Brunel and the board has decided to extend the maximum age for mixed football to under 16."

One last season playing with the boys! I'd become the first ever girl in England to play mixed football through to under 16 and *still* get to sign for Huddersfield. From my point of view that was the perfect ending.

And so it was.

My final season in junior football was definitely the best. Things seemed to be coming together. I was selected to represent the County for a second season and was also made captain. At Ireland I graduated from the under 16 team and was called up twice for the under 17 squad. I also found a new boys' team too without any trouble.

Newly promoted Beighton Magpies were looking for a right-back, so I signed for them. I'm so glad I did because it was the best mixed-football experience I'd ever had. The coach, Steve Featherstone, was great, and the team was pretty good too. It was much more straightforward than any trial I'd had before. They were obviously a bit surprised when I turned up, but they knew where I'd been playing and there was no sniggering at all. In fact, they actually seemed quite pleased to see me. The trial went so well, Steve asked me if I'd be willing to sign about 10 minutes into the practice game.

"You're a good player. We're short of a right-back and I think having you will be a great influence on the rest of the team."

Steve called the players round during a break and told them I'd agreed to sign. They all gave me a round of applause, which felt great. He told them he didn't want anyone treating me different because I was a girl. He needn't have bothered. Everybody at the club was sound from that first practice session onwards.

I settled in immediately. I was 'Player of the Game' in my second match, and made captain in my third. It was the first time I'd ever captained a boys' team. It was a really tough league. We didn't win every week, but we were always competitive, usually in games until right at the end, and had lots of memorable matches and some great results.

I was also made captain for my second season with the County. The previous year, I'd been playing a year up but this time I was in the right age group. At County matches the boys' and girls' teams – and different age groups – play at the same time. I didn't really know many of the girls, but I recognised almost all of the boys from teams I'd played against. I'd even played in the same side as one of them.

The County is run very formally. The three captains (under 16 girls and under 16 and under 18 boys) are expected to arrive early, meet the opposition off the coach and show them to the changing rooms. Before one game I got chatting to the under 16 captain, Spencer. He was a decent guy, so I asked him what team he played for.

"Handsworth," he replied.

"Ah, I thought I recognised you," I said. " I play for Beighton."

A couple of the other lads overheard our conversation.

"Wait, are you that girl who plays in our league?"

"Do you remember playing us? You decked our left-winger."

Suddenly we were all remembering games we'd played against each other and were swapping stories. Somebody else said he played for Handsworth, and he remembered beating me when I played for Dronfield.

"I remember you. We beat you 4-0 in the cup last year," he said.

"Yeah I remember you too," I replied. "I used to play for Millhouses as well. Do you also remember when we beat you 3-0 at your place?"

Everyone started killing themselves laughing.

"You actually beat Handsworth? Millhouses were a right team."

It's not often you get to take the mickey out of Handsworth.

It turned out I'd played against one lad the week before. He was called James, a midfielder for Wombwell who were top of the league. The game had finished in a 4-4 draw.

"We turned up and the whole team was looking at you going 'What are we supposed to do? Are we supposed to tackle her or just leave her?'" he said. "There was a 50/50 between us just after the kick-off and I remember thinking, 'I can't lose this, I'll have the piss taken out of me!' But you went straight in for it and absolutely clattered me. I couldn't believe it!"

The match against Wombwell had been particularly memorable for two reasons. Firstly because I scored a goal and secondly because Dr Laura Hills came to watch me play. Although we had spoken on the phone, this was the first time we had actually met. I was flattered that Dr Hills was prepared to make a seven-hour round trip to see me play and I was also looking forward to shaking hands with the woman who had made this all possible. I really wanted to make sure I did well and, in that respect, getting a goal while she was watching was brilliant. It was also very lucky as I didn't score another all season

After the match Dr Hills told me more about her research findings. The mixed gender project was now into its seventh year and there was compelling evidence that mixed football worked very well for some girls.

"And I'm delighted that the barriers are finally being removed as a result of girls like you," she said.

It was so good to meet someone in a position of authority who was entirely positive about mixed football. I felt that I was finally able to get my views across and that Dr Hills was genuinely interested in what I had to say. She also put me in touch with one of her research students who interviewed me about my experiences a few days later.

A lot of Dr Hills' research concerned the issue of how girls coped with the increasing physicality of the boys' game. I did find boys' football at under 16s a lot more challenging physically than any other level I had played, but I think that's also true for boys. The big difference however is that girls hit puberty earlier than boys. At Millhouses I'd been one of the tallest players, but my growth spurt had finished while the boys' was just starting. So, just two years later, I was still 5ft 7in, but now one of the smaller players. At Beighton our centre-backs, Rio and Harry, were 6ft 3in and 6ft 2in, while Josh, who played up front, was 6ft 7in. Winning headers was never easy. I also had to adapt to the fact that the lads were not just bigger, but faster too. I was still more than holding my own though. I started every game and the thrill of winning a 50/50 never wore thin.

Yet despite the fact that it was harder I was enjoying it more than ever, both on and off the pitch. I didn't know whether it was because the lads were a bit older and slightly more mature, but under 16 was the first time I'd had proper mates in the team: friends who I would talk to outside of football.

One team-mate even asked for my advice about whether he should get his hair cut. He sent me through a picture of Joey Essex. I said I thought it would suit him. He said thanks because he thought so too, but when he'd asked his other mates, they'd said they thought he'd look like a dickhead.

But it wasn't just the boys in my team who were reacting differently. By now I was used to wingers trying to impose themselves on the game in the first few minutes. They'd usually try and go in really hard for the first header or shove me at the throw-in. Dad said they used to call it 'letting them know you're there.' It was as if they were trying to show me it was a man's game. I didn't know how they expected me to respond, perhaps they thought they were the first person to try this tactic. This season though, sometimes things were different.

In one game, there was a really strong crosswind, and most of the play in the early stages was down the opposite side of the pitch. As the ball went out for another throw-in, the winger I was marking turned round and said, "I was just wondering how come you play for a boys' team?"

"I just prefer it," I said

"That's interesting. Have you ever played with girls?"

"Yes, I used to play at an academy, but... erm the ball's coming."

"Oh yeah, right. I was just interested."

My dad shouted something at me from the touchline about not getting forward enough. I told him to shut up.

"Oh, is that your Dad?" asked the winger.

"Erm, yes it is," I said.

"What does he think about you playing with boys? Is he quite supportive?"

I was confused. I was sweaty, covered in mud, it was raining and my hair was tied up and plastered down, yet this boy was obviously trying to spark up a conversation.

That had never happened before. He seemed really nice, but I think I'd have found it easier to deal with if he'd been trying to intimidate me like normal.

We had a good run in the Tesco Cup, a national competition for under 16 teams. After coming through the earlier rounds we were drawn against a team from the A League, and what was always going to be a tough game was made especially hard by the fact we only had 11 fit players. Steve reckoned that our best chance of scoring would come from a set piece. We had four players over 6ft tall, so the plan was to throw them into the box for corners, free kicks and throw-ins. Corners are all about making runs, getting your arms up and ensuring you're the one who gets a head on the ball. I was now one of the smaller players in the team but, though my chances of winning a header were slim, I still had a fairly important job to do. I was to stand in front of the keeper and try to drag him out of position towards the near post. Luke would then play the cross into the back post, where Josh and Kiann would be arriving to head it in.

If the keeper did what he was supposed to, which is ignore me and stand his ground, then the plan didn't work, but a lot of them found it really distracting having to mark a girl. I normally leaned back into them so they shoved me forwards, and then I kept doing that but would edge forwards each time so they didn't notice I was actually dragging them towards the front post. It didn't work every single time, but it was a good tactic and got us plenty of goals.

We were defending for most of the match, but we kept hitting them on the break and won a lot of corners. My tactic of marking the keeper was soon noticed. As soon as I started to run into position they'd start shouting out, "Here she comes again, Jack!", "She likes you, Jack!", "She's got something for you, Jack!"

This team was from a small town, the sort of place where everyone knows everyone else.

"Yeah lads," said Jack, "It's like Olivia last night, isn't it?"

They all laughed, but the plan was working: Jack wasn't staying in position. Despite what he was saying, I could see he was finding my presence really distracting. He was focused on pushing me in the back really hard to make a point to his team-mates rather than concentrating on the corners. He didn't realise that this was part of the plan. One time I thought I might get a penalty so I went down, but at that point the ref told me to stop backing in.

Another corner...

"Here she comes again, Jack. She's back for more!"

We went close. First we hit the bar, and then another was headed off the line. Eventually, with eight minutes to go, the tactic worked and Josh got his goal, taking the game to extra time. We finished with only 10 players and ended up losing, but we'd run them close for most of the match.

After it was over I didn't really give the game much more thought. But the next day when I got home from school and checked Facebook, I had three new friend requests – all from boys who'd been at the game the previous day. One of them hadn't even been playing in the match, so I guessed this was probably some kind of dare. Sure enough, the spectator had sent me a screenshot of their group chat, which was really funny. It said, 'AND SHE PLAYS FOR IRELAND!!!' followed by a smiley face with love heart eyes. Underneath was a comment saying, 'My friend really likes you.'

A few minutes later another message came through, this one from the goalkeeper I'd been marking. He said, 'Ignore my friend, he's being an idiot. But well played yesterday...'

People always ask me whether I think boys are better footballers than girls. To me that's like asking if men are better than women. Mia Hamm says you need stamina, strength and speed to become a top player. Of course, you need other things as well, but without these foundations in place you won't make it. Men are always going to be stronger, faster and bigger – that's the way they're made – but that doesn't mean they're all better. I'll never be quick enough or strong enough to play in the Premier League or the Football League, but neither will any of the boys I've played against for that matter, or 99.99 per cent of all the other boys playing in this country. But that's not the point. It's simply about being able to compete at whatever level you play at. Girls are proving that they can compete with boys in junior football. I might be the first, but I definitely won't be the last and who can say how far they will get in the future, once all the barriers have been removed.

Sometimes at the weekend when there are other matches going on I'll see girls playing with lads in the younger age groups. They're usually pretty good. My brother played in the Under 14 County Cup semi-final this year and there was a girl playing in the other semi-final. I am confident that this will be a common sight in the future and I look forward to seeing teams with two or three girls doing really well.

I now coach the under 9 girls' team at Sheffield Wednesday. We've got a good squad but one player also plays for a boys' team. You can see the difference it makes. Girls like her will now be able to play for their teams all the way through, if they choose to do so, without having to stress about being excluded at the end of the season.

I think that this will be good for the women's game too. Not only will it improve the girls as players, but it will change men's attitudes as well and that will only help perceptions of the women's game. I don't think many of the boys I've played with would say that girls can't play football.

Epilogue

"I want to win FIFA's best goal award for my skill - not my sex."
Stephanie Roche, Irish footballer, shortlisted for FIFA's goal of the year 2015

On 18th December 2014 I was on my way to school when I received a text from Glen Preston, the Huddersfield Town manager:

David,

Niamh McKevitt is now 16. Is there any chance we can get her signed now in time for Sunday's game? (I've copied Niamh and her dad in).

Cheers,
Glen

Dad and Glen spent the rest of morning running around trying to get the paperwork sorted. At one point it all seemed like it might be all off. Somebody thought that I'd need international clearance from the FAI, which would slow everything down, but thankfully it didn't. I was oblivious to all this, because I was sat in lessons. At lunchtime I turned on my phone and found another text. This time from Dad:

Congratulations!
You are officially a Huddersfield Town player. Glen has
said you'll be starting on Sunday. He's going to send a
tactics video through. Well done, Niamh. Don't forget to
empty the dishwasher when you get in.

Dad
x

And that was how I found out, five days after my 16th birthday, that I had actually achieved my ambition and signed for a Premier League club. I wonder if this is how it happened for Gareth Bale or Harry Kane?

My final match for Beighton was a 5-4 victory against my old club Dronfield Town. A thrilling game played in a brilliant atmosphere: it was the perfect way to end my time in mixed football.

But the season wasn't over for me. I immediately started training twice a week with Huddersfield who, due to poor winter weather and postponements, still had around a dozen games to play. I was soon combining fighting for a place in the first team with revising for my GCSEs.

Within a month, I got my chance. On 21st March 2015, I made my Women's Premier League debut away at West Brom (S.C. Albion). I came off the bench and played right-midfield in a 1-0 victory. There wasn't much time to celebrate, however, as on the journey home I had to get on with my French revision.

I finished the season with seven first-team appearances. I'm really enjoying playing women's football and have already had several memorable moments. In a friendly against Doncaster Belles, I was responsible for marking Sue Smith, who was capped 93 times for England. I also played in a cup final: a 3-1 defeat to Sheffield FC, sadly. My P.E teacher, Miss Giampalma, was playing for them. I think she was quite surprised to see me lining up for the opposition in the handshake saying, "Alright Miss."

We ended the season with a 4-0 demolition of Preston. It was probably the best team performance I've ever been involved in and meant we finished the league in fifth place. It was a night match, away from home, on the evening before my English Literature paper, so there was yet more revision in the car.

Sheffield FC went on to win the Premier League play-off (Miss Giampalma scored the winner in extra time) and were promoted to the Women's Super League. My aims for next season are to help Huddersfield Town follow them there and to play well enough to be called up for the Ireland squad again. One thing is certain though: I will definitely be captaining the South Yorkshire County Under 17s on a tour of the USA in 2016.

My dream is still to play football in the USA and that is beginning to look like it might be possible. I have been invited to Germany to take part in trials for US college scholarships (although that does mean I've got to spend the summer after my GCSEs studying for the entrance exam). So even though my experience with boys' football has come to an end, there's still a lot to look forward to.

On the 21st May 2015, the FA announced that the age limit for mixed football would be raised to under 18s. I am pleased that girls coming through will now have a chance to play at that level if they want to and I'm proud to have been able to play a very small part in getting the rules changed. I hope my story inspires other girls to try mixed football. I love playing the game, whether it's been with men or women, boys or girls.

For me it was always just about playing football at the highest level that I could. For a long time that was in boys' football, but now my future is in the women's game. But wherever I'm playing, it's all just football to me.